# Season's Greetings

# A Play

## Alan Ayckbourn

*Samuel French — London*

*New York — Sydney — Toronto — Hollywood*

# SEASON'S GREETINGS

First presented at the Stephen Joseph Theatre in the Round, Scarborough, on 25th September 1980, with the following cast of characters:

| | |
|---|---|
| **Neville** | Michael Simkins |
| **Belinda,** his wife | Tessa Peake-Jones |
| **Phyllis,** his sister | Susan Uebel |
| **Harvey,** his uncle | Robin Herford |
| **Bernard,** Phyllis's husband | Ronald Herdman |
| **Rachel,** Belinda's sister | Marcia Warren |
| **Eddie** | Jeffrey Robert |
| **Pattie,** Eddie's wife | Lavinia Bertram |
| **Clive** | Robin Bowerman |

Subsequently presented at the Apollo Theatre, London, by Michael Codron in the Greenwich Theatre production on 29th March 1982, with the following cast of characters:

| | |
|---|---|
| **Neville** | Bryan Marshall |
| **Belinda** | Barbara Ferris |
| **Phyllis** | Bridget Turner |
| **Harvey** | Peter Vaughan |
| **Bernard** | Bernard Hepton |
| **Rachel** | Marcia Warren |
| **Eddie** | Brian Hall |
| **Pattie** | Diane Bull |
| **Clive** | Christopher Strauli |

The play directed by Alan Ayckbourn
Setting by Edward Lipscomb

The action takes place in the home of Neville and Belinda Bunker

ACT I    SCENE 1    Christmas Eve, 7.30 p.m.
          SCENE 2    Christmas Day, noon
          SCENE 3    Christmas Day, midnight

ACT II    SCENE 1    Boxing Day, 3.30 p.m.
          SCENE 2    December 27th, 5.15 a.m.

Time—the present

# ACT I

## SCENE 1

*The home of Neville and Belinda Bunker. Christmas Eve, 7.30 p.m.*

*It is a six-bedroomed, three storey-plus-attic, modern house. Well kept, without being too trendy or ultra tasteful, it also has that clear appearance of a house containing young children. Our view is of the ground floor and is dominated by the front hall though this is not of any particular size or magnificence, larger than some, rectangular with a main staircase leading off upstairs. Besides the front door, there are two other doors: one opening on to a dining-room, the other to the sitting-room. The hall is furnished with an upright chair beside a telephone table which also has on it a table lamp. On the other side of the hall is a small carved wooden bench, and just inside the front door a coat- and umbrella-stand. Near the foot of the stairs, currently dominating everything, is a large Christmas tree, eight or nine feet high standing in a substantial tub. The tree is festooned with decorative bulbs but has not yet been fully dressed. Arranged around the base are a large number of presents, brightly gift wrapped and labelled. Also leading off the hall is a kitchen passageway. This runs alongside the dining-room, and possibly contains a hatchway through to it. The dining-room itself is apparently large though our view of it is restricted. We see probably a third, including some of a sideboard and a third of what must be a very long dining-table. We see only one end of this, including the chair at the top and a maximum of two further chairs on each side. Similarly, we see only a portion of the sitting-room. This includes a window with window-seat, a single armchair with side-table. This chair faces away towards an unseen fire and an unseen television set. We can gather again from, amongst other things, the floor covering that this room too is fairly big*

*The house glows warm and cosy: a wonderful place for children or adults to spend Christmas. At the start, Harvey Bunker, a man in his sixties, with cropped hair and a slightly military appearance, is seated in the sitting-room armchair watching the off-stage television. He is immensely enjoying an old adventure film and laughs uproariously at something he is watching. In a moment, Dr Bernard Longstaff, a rather faded man in his forties comes pattering downstairs. He carries about half a dozen gift-wrapped presents. He reaches the bottom of the stairs, looks round and sees no-one. Then, hearing Harvey laughing, he goes to the sitting-room doorway and stands looking at the television screen*

**Harvey** This is a marvellous film, you know. Marvellous.

**Bernard** I think I've seen it before, haven't I?

**Harvey** (*slightly irritably*) What's that?

**Bernard** I said, I have a feeling that this film's been on TV before. Hasn't it?

**Harvey** Probably. I think it was on last Christmas.

**Bernard** Ah.

**Harvey** Matter of fact, I think it's on every Christmas. It's very old.

**Barnard** Oh yes.

**Harvey** He's dead now. That one there.

**Bernard** Yes.

**Harvey** And him. He's definitely dead. He died not long ago.

**Bernard** And her.

**Harvey** Oh, yes, she's dead. She's been dead for years.

**Bernard** Yes, I can remember her dying.

**Harvey** I don't know about this chap.

**Bernard** No.

*They both stare at the screen*

**Harvey** I could be wrong, I think I read somewhere he's in a home. Alcoholic.

**Bernard** Oh dear.

*They watch again. Harvey laughs*

**Harvey** Damn fine film though. Even if they are all dead.

*At this moment, Belinda, an attractive woman in her early thirties, comes downstairs. She is carrying some large boxes containing Christmas decorations for the tree. As she comes down, she calls back to the children behind her that she hears but we do not*

**Belinda** Not unless you go to sleep, you won't. You do as Pattie tells you and go to sleep . . .

*A child apparently says something*

Go to sleep. (*She puts the boxes by the tree*)

*Bernard, on hearing her, comes out of the sitting-room*

**Bernard** Er . . .

**Belinda** Bernard?

**Bernard** (*indicating his pile of parcels*) All right if I put these . . .?

**Belinda** With the others? Of course. We're going to do the usual thing. Give the kids their stockings tomorrow morning with some little things and save the big presents for Boxing Day.

*Belinda goes off along the kitchen passageway*

**Bernard** Right, yes. That's—er—that's best. Yes. (*He arranges his parcels around the foot of the tree with the others*)

**Harvey** (*still watching the television*) Bang! Look at that. Blown them to smithereens. Ought to have the kids down to watch this. Just up their street. Next time you do one of your shows for them, Bernard, take my tip. Put a bit of blood in it. They'll love it.

**Bernard** (*unconvinced*) Oh—hardly . . .
**Harvey** For God's sake, get them used to real life, man. You're a doctor, you ought to appreciate that. Give them some guts.
**Bernard** (*muttering*) I'm sorry, we don't agree, Harvey, we really don't. I'm sorry.
**Harvey** (*back at the television screen*) Boom! There goes another one.
**Bernard** We never have. It's a vicious spiral. You introduce children to violence in adults and the next thing you know, they're——
**Harvey** Well, I'll tell you this . . .
**Bernard** —imitating them . . .
**Harvey** I'll tell you what I've given them all for Christmas and I'm not ashamed to say so. I've given them all a gun. All except Gary who's got a crossbow because he had a gun last year. But Lydia, Katie, Flora and Zoe, they're not getting any of your wee-weeing dollies and nurses' uniforms from me. They've all got guns, so there.
**Bernard** Well, I'm sorry, I think that is irresponsible and if I were a parent, I would . . .
**Harvey** But you're not, Bernard, you're not and that's your trouble. You've got no kids and you don't know a bloody thing about them.
**Bernard** I'm not arguing, Harvey, I am not arguing. We have this discussion every Christmas and I am not going to be drawn into it again. We beg to differ.

*Belinda returns from the kitchen with a small stepladder*

**Belinda** Now, what's going on?
**Bernard** Nothing. Nothing.
**Belinda** (*setting down the steps by the tree*) I don't want any of that, please. The holiday has only just started and I can do without that.
**Bernard** (*sulkily*) I should speak to Harvey, not me.
**Harvey** (*calling out through the sitting-room door*) Aha, wait till you see what I've got you for Christmas.
**Bernard** Me?
**Harvey** Yes, you.
**Bernard** What?
**Harvey** Aha. Something to wake your ideas up. You'll see.
**Bernard** If it's another of your awful jokes, I'd prefer not to have it.
**Belinda** Bernard, Phyllis wants you in the kitchen.
**Bernard** (*immediately concerned*) Is she all right?
**Belinda** She seems to be. There's a lot of steam and groaning but I think she's coping.
**Bernard** (*hurrying off*) I'd better see what she wants.

*Bernard goes off to the kitchen*

*Belinda, about to decorate the tree, goes to the sitting-room doorway*

**Belinda** All right, Harvey?
**Harvey** (*totally absorbed*) Bel, look at this. Watch this bit.
**Belinda** Oh yes. Haven't I seen this?

**Harvey** Ah. There he goes. That's—er—what? That's a sixty-foot fall, that. Sensational.

**Belinda** Haven't you got a drink yet?

**Harvey** No.

**Belinda** Well, where the hell's Neville? He was fetching us all a drink an hour ago. What were you having?

**Harvey** A small ginger wine, please.

**Belinda** Ginger wine. Still in training?

**Harvey** Like to keep fit, you know, Bel. I'll have a drop of wine at dinner.

**Belinda** If we get it. Phyllis is out there in the throes.

**Harvey** Oh good God. Drunk in charge of an oven . . .

**Belinda** Ssh! (*She goes to the dining-room doorway. Calling into the room*) Nev? Neville . . . (*She goes to the foot of the stairs. Puzzled*) They haven't gone out, have they? (*She moves to the front door*) Nev, where are you? Nev?

*Pattie, a woman of about thirty, appears at the top of the stairs. She is noticeably seven months pregnant*

**Pattie** Ssh.

**Belinda** Pattie, I'm sorry. Are they asleep?

**Pattie** All except Gary. Is Eddie down there?

**Belinda** Well, he's probably wherever Neville is but I've lost Neville. If they've gone to the pub . . .

**Pattie** Could you ask Eddie to come up? Gary won't go to sleep until he sees Eddie.

**Belinda** OK. Would you like a drink?

**Pattie** Oh yes. Oh yes, a drink. Lovely. Why not?

*Pattie goes off upstairs*

**Belinda** Well, what would you . . . (*She shrugs and gives up*)

*Bernard comes back from the kitchen with nine place mats. He has some flour on him*

Bernard, is Nev in the kitchen?

**Bernard** No, just Phyllis.

**Belinda** Well, where are Nev and Eddie?

**Bernard** I don't know. They may be out in the . . .

**Belinda** You all right, you look pale?

**Bernard** No, I think it's flour.

**Belinda** Flour?

**Bernard** Cornflour. Phyllis dropped a tin of cornflour. It flew up in a cloud. It's all right, it's under control.

**Belinda** (*unsure*) Oh yes?

**Bernard** It was just a little dizzy spell. She's over it. She's coping. Don't worry . . .

*Bernard goes into the dining-room and begins laying out the place mats. Belinda follows him and starts rummaging in the sideboard cupboard for drinks*

**Belinda** (*as she does so*) Look, if she'd rather I carried on for her.
**Bernard** No. No. She's all right, really. It's good she's doing this. It
really is.
**Belinda** Not if she's fainting all over my kitchen ...

*Neville, an easy-going man in his late thirties, enters along the kitchen
passageway. He is followed by Eddie. Eddie is less successful, less at ease
than Neville whom he obviously admires, or at least requires. Neville
carries a small, home-made remote radio control box, similar to the type
used to control TV sets, but this with only two buttons*

**Neville** (*as they enter*) Personally, I find every single claim they make can
be taken with a huge pinch of salt and that includes their frequency
response details which are pie-in-the-sky to start with, because I have
personally tested every single speaker of theirs we have ever had in
stock and they've got to be joking.
**Eddie** Really, really?
**Neville** It's all never-never-land and hallo-Hong Kong, I can tell you.
**Belinda** (*coming out of the dining-room to meet them*) Nev, where have you
been?
**Neville** My darling.
**Belinda** (*holding up an empty ginger wine bottle*) Have we any more of
this?
**Neville** We are awash.
**Belinda** Where is it?
**Neville** Out the back.
**Belinda** Would you fetch it, please?
**Neville** (*taking the empty bottle from her*) My pleasure.
**Belinda** And could you also do all those lovely drinks you promised
everyone half an hour ago?
**Neville** Of course, of course.
**Belinda** Otherwise I'll never get this tree done.

*Bernard comes out of the dining-room and goes through the hall and back
into the kitchen*

(*Moving the steps into position*) It's a ginger wine for Uncle Harvey,
and a something or other, she didn't say, for Pattie.
**Neville** Right. (*He goes into the dining-room, and takes out an ice bucket*)
**Eddie** Pattie never knows. Don't bother asking her.
**Belinda** And she also wants you up there, Eddie.
**Eddie** Right. (*He does not move, but watches Belinda*)
**Neville** Eddie, could you do these while I get some more of this, please?
**Eddie** Fine.
**Neville** (*going to the kitchen*) I'll have a Scotch.
**Eddie** Fine.
**Belinda** (*after Neville*) And some ice.

*Neville goes off with the ginger wine bottle and the ice bucket*

*Belinda starts to decorate the tree. During the following Eddie, unable to find any ginger wine, pours a ginger ale. Then he finds a bottle of Scotch and pours out two of these*

**Harvey** (*calling out*) Hey, you're missing a first-rate shark fight in here.
**Belinda** (*busy with her decoration*) Oh dear.
**Harvey** Killer sharks.

*Pattie appears at the top of the stairs*

**Pattie** Belinda, is Eddie down there?
**Belinda** (*from her ladder*) Eddie?
**Eddie** (*from the dining-room*) Hallo.
**Belinda** Pattie wants you.
**Eddie** (*continuing pouring his drinks*) What does she want?
**Belinda** What do you want, he says.
**Pattie** Can he come up?
**Belinda** Can you come up, she says.
**Eddie** In a minute.
**Belinda** In a minute.
**Pattie** Well, Gary won't go to sleep till he's seen him. He doesn't believe he's here. Tell him I don't want to sit up in this bedroom all night. I want to come down and have a drink.

*Pattie goes off upstairs*

**Belinda** Yes, well what are you going to have to . . . (*She sees that Pattie has gone*) Oh.
**Eddie** What's that?
**Belinda** Nothing. Just trying to find out what she wanted.
**Eddie** (*drily*) If she tells you, let me know, won't you?

*Belinda continues to decorate the tree. It is a task she enjoys*

**Harvey** You've just missed a damn fine shark fight, you lot.
**Belinda** (*abstractedly*) Oh, what a pity. That's a wonderful bit, too.

*Eddie comes to the dining-room doorway*

**Eddie** Nev's just been showing me his workshop out the back there.
**Belinda** Oh yes?
**Eddie** He's got himself nicely set up now then, eh?
**Belinda** Yes.
**Eddie** Marvellous. All those power tools. I envy him those power tools.
**Belinda** Yes, it's good to see where the money goes. It's all invested in a shed round the back of the house.
**Eddie** Ah, don't be like that. Man's got to have a hobby, hasn't he?
**Belinda** Why?
**Eddie** Well . . . (*He is momentarily floored*) He just does. He's got to get away, hasn't he?
**Belinda** Away from what?
**Eddie** Well. Everything.
**Belinda** Me?

**Eddie** I didn't say that.
**Belinda** Obviously me. What else? Me and the kids.
**Eddie** Well, I'm saying nothing. You take that up with Nev.
**Belinda** I would. Except I never see him. He's always in his bloody shed.

*Eddie retreats back into the dining-room and finishes pouring the drinks*

**Eddie** (*muttering to himself as he does so*) Man's got to have a hobby.

*Bernard comes through with some side plates from the kitchen*

**Bernard** Er . . .
**Belinda** (*without turning round*) Bernard?
**Bernard** Phyllis wants to know how many of us there's going to be.
**Belinda** I've told her. Nine.
**Bernard** I mean to say this man is definite, is he? This Clive Thing man is definitely coming?
**Belinda** According to Rachel, he is. She's gone to the station to meet him.
**Bernard** She just didn't seem all that certain.
**Belinda** Well, he's coming as far as I know. Phyllis all right, is she? Dropped anything else?
**Bernard** No, she's—well, as a matter of fact, she's having a little nose bleed. It's not serious. She's lying down. She'll be fine.
**Belinda** (*mildly alarmed*) Are you sure?
**Bernard** Yes. When she felt dizzy, she straightened up too quickly, you see and she banged her head on the cupboard. It's only a nose bleed.
**Belinda** Lord . . . (*She continues decorating*)

*Bernard goes into the dining-room and starts to lay out his place mats*

**Harvey** (*laughing to himself*) Hah! He made short work of him.
**Eddie** (*to Bernard*) Do you want a drink, Bernard?
**Bernard** No, I'd better get all this done first, thank you, Eddie.
**Eddie** You—er . . . Are you going to be doing your Christmas play again this year, Bernard?
**Bernard** My puppet show? Oh yes. On Boxing Day as usual. I think I'm doing it whether I like it or not. It's become rather traditional, hasn't it? Uncle Bernard and his puppets. (*He laughs*)
**Eddie** (*laughing too*) Yes. It just occurred to me, Bernard, you know, just a thought—maybe you might be thinking of jazzing it up a bit this year. I mean, I know it's a puppet show and you can't obviously do that much, I mean with all those strings and so on, but just make the story a bit more zippy, if you know what I mean? I think the kids would appreciate that. I know our three would. You should see the things they watch on TV these days. You don't mind me saying this?
**Bernard** (*icily*) Has Harvey put you up to this?
**Eddie** No, no.
**Bernard** I will continue to do my puppet plays as I wish to do them and as I know children enjoy them. I think you know that I will always accept help with the manipulation but I will not have people interfering with the content of my plays. I refuse to pander. I will not include

gratuitous violence or sex. Not for anyone. I will not do that. I'm sorry.

**Eddie** Who's talking about sex? I didn't mention sex.

**Bernard** I know exactly what you're talking about, don't worry.

**Eddie** I don't know why you bring sex into it.

**Bernard** I thought as a parent you might have been a little more responsible.

**Eddie** All right. All right. (*He walks into the hall with the ginger ale*) I did not speak. I never spoke.

**Bernard** (*leaving the dining-room and returning to the kitchen*) I'm disappointed, that's all I can say, I'm disappointed.

*Bernard goes to the kitchen*

**Belinda** What's going on?

**Eddie** All I did was mention his puppet show.

**Belinda** He's very touchy. Especially after last year.

**Eddie** Maybe. Maybe. But someone's got to tell him. I mean, if he does another show like last year the kids will mutiny. Gary threatened not to come at all.

**Belinda** He always has so much scenery. It takes hours just changing the scenery and then it always falls down. Poor Bernard.

**Eddie** We'll have to do something.

*Eddie goes towards the sitting-room*

*Simultaneously, Neville returns along the kitchen passageway with a new bottle of ginger wine and a full ice bucket*

*Eddie stops in the sitting-room doorway*

**Neville** What are we having for supper?

**Belinda** Roast lamb, I think. Why?

**Neville** I just wondered. Phyllis is lying stretched out on the kitchen table with three yards of kitchen towel stuck up her nose, I just wondered. (*He goes into the dining-room*)

**Eddie** (*laughing and going into the sitting-room*) Here we are Harvey, one glass of lovely ginger.

**Harvey** Thank you. Watch this. (*He indicates the television set*)

*Eddie stands and watches*

**Belinda** So long as she's coping.

**Neville** (*placing the ginger wine bottle and the ice on the sideboard*) Phyllis?

**Belinda** Yes.

**Neville** (*coming out of the dining-room*) Well. She's obviously been drinking but she's no worse than usual.

**Belinda** Where'd she get it from? I haven't given her a drink.

**Neville** I haven't. (*As an afterthought*) Ah. Hang on. I opened her some red wine to put in the gravy.

**Belinda** Look, we really must stop this business of her cooking the Christmas Eve meal, you know. It's beyond a joke. I mean, all right, I know she's your sister but all the same . . .

**Neville** (*shrugging*) Well, it's Christmas. (*He goes back into the dining-room and puts ice in his and Eddie's glasses*)
**Eddie** (*staring at the screen*) I haven't seen this for ages. It's good this.
**Harvey** Marvellous film. Marvellous. Look at him there . . . That's it. Down he goes. We could do with this chap round Clapham Common. He'd sort the little bastards out. Cheers.
**Eddie** Cheers.
**Harvey** (*trying his drink and choking*) What's this?
**Eddie** Ginger thing . . .
**Harvey** Ginger ale.
**Eddie** Right. Ginger ale. Ah, now you wanted ginger wine, didn't you?
**Harvey** Course I wanted ginger wine.
**Eddie** Right.
**Harvey** I don't want ginger ale.
**Eddie** No, ginger wine. That's what you want.
**Harvey** Ginger wine.
**Eddie** Right.

*Bernard returns with the cruet*

*Eddie, seeing him, lingers in the sitting-room doorway. He drinks the rest of the ginger ale and watches the television. Bernard goes into the dining-room*

**Bernard** I mean, I'm not perfect for heaven's sake, I know that.
**Neville** (*turning somewhat startled*) What?
**Bernard** But I do try. Every day, I try. And nowhere do I try more than with that woman out there in that kitchen. With my dear wife. With Phyllis. I've given everything I have for that woman's health and I'd give more. I really would, believe me, Neville.
**Neville** (*gently*) Bernard, what are you talking about?
**Bernard** I'm just—trying to explain . . .
**Neville** You don't have to explain to us, Bernard, we know. We all know. We've seen what you've . . .
**Bernard** (*going out*) I have to explain to someone. Sometimes. I need to.

*Bernard goes off into the kitchen*

*Belinda, on her ladder, turns*

**Neville** He's getting worse.
**Belinda** Is he going to be in that state all over Christmas?
**Eddie** (*going into the dining-room*) That's my fault, that is.
**Neville** What did you do?

*Eddie puts the empty ginger ale glass on the sideboard. He finds his Scotch, now with ice, and sips it*

**Eddie** I mentioned his puppet show to him.
**Neville** Oh no, he's not doing another one, is he?
**Belinda** Of course.
**Neville** Well I, for one, shall be out.
**Belinda** Nev.

**Neville** No, I'm sorry. I'm not sitting through another one of those, I'm sorry. Ali-Baba last year was my lot. Forty thieves and they all came on with ten minute intervals between them.
**Belinda** Neville.
**Neville** No way. (*He toasts Eddie*) Cheers.
**Eddie** (*responding*) Cheers.
**Neville** Happy Christmas.
**Eddie** Yes.
**Belinda** Thanks very much. I don't get one, then?
**Eddie** Oh.
**Neville** Didn't know you wanted one.
**Belinda** Probably because you didn't ask me.

*During the following, Eddie pours a ginger wine for Harvey, using the same glass*

**Neville** My darling, I'm not psychic. If you'd said something . . .
**Belinda** My darling, you only had to ask me . . .
**Neville** All right, I'm asking you now.
**Belinda** You just have to ask, that's all. "Darling, would you like a drink?"
**Neville** Darling, would you like a drink, I'm asking you—
**Belinda** —then you'd find out, wouldn't you?
**Neville** Would you like a drink darling, I'm asking you now? Would you like a bloody drink? Yes or no?
**Belinda** Yes, please. I'll have a gin.
**Neville** Thank you so, so much.
**Eddie** (*coming out of the dining-room carrying the ginger wine*) I'll get it.
**Neville** Thank you, Eddie.

*Eddie turns to go back into the dining-room*

**Belinda** No, you won't. He'll get it.
**Neville** I'll get it. What's the difference?
**Belinda** The difference is you are getting me something for a change. That's the difference.
**Neville** All right.
**Eddie** (*cheerfully, as he crosses the hall to the sitting-room*) Now, we don't want to start Christmas like this, do we?

*Pattie appears at the top of the stairs*

**Pattie** Eddie, are you coming up or aren't you?
**Eddie** (*savagely*) In a minute. In a minute.
**Pattie** (*hurt*) All right.

*Pattie goes back*

**Eddie** (*apologetically to the others*) I'm doing this, aren't I? (*He goes into the sitting-room*)
**Harvey** (*calling out*) We're just getting to the bit with the avalanche, if anyone's interested.
**Belinda** Super, that's a lovely bit.

**Eddie** (*crossing to Harvey*) Great. Here you are, Harvey, try this.

*Harvey takes the glass and sniffs it suspiciously*

**Neville** (*brightly*) I'm putting your drink here for you, darling. (*He places it on the hall table*)

**Belinda** Thank you so much, darling. (*She continues trimming the tree*)

*Neville now has the remote-control box again. Eddie is again crossing the sitting-room back to the door, his eyes fixed on the television set*

**Neville** Hey, Eddie, I was going to show you this.

**Eddie** (*without moving*) Oh yes, show me that.

*Rachel comes in through the front door. She is a little older than her sister Belinda and less conventionally pretty. Just now, she is trying to give an expression of extreme normality but is in fact deeply anxious*

*Belinda and Neville turn to her expectantly. She smiles back*

**Belinda** (*impatiently*) Well?

**Rachel** Well.

**Belinda** Where is he?

**Rachel** He wasn't on the train. (*She starts to take off her coat*)

**Belinda** Oh no. Wasn't on it?

**Rachel** No.

**Belinda** Does that mean he's not coming?

**Rachel** No idea.

**Neville** He might be on the eight-oh-five.

**Rachel** I somehow doubt it.

**Belinda** Yes, if he missed the seven-thirty, he'll probably be on the eight-oh-five.

**Rachel** If he'd missed the seven-thirty, he'd've rung.

**Belinda** Possibly. But then again, he might . . .

**Rachel** It really doesn't matter.

*Rachel hurries upstairs*

**Belinda** If he'd missed the seven-thirty and had to hurry——

**Rachel** It's really of no interest to me one way or the other.

**Belinda** It is to me. After we spent most of the day clearing that attic out for him . . .

*Rachel goes off upstairs*

*Eddie comes out of the sitting-room*

Oh.

**Neville** Lost her writer, has she?

**Belinda** Apparently.

**Eddie** What does he write, then?

**Belinda** Books.

**Eddie** Oh, yes . . .

**Neville** I've never heard of him. (*To Eddie*) Have you ever heard of him?

**Eddie** No, I've never heard of anybody.

**Belinda** His book's by our bed, why don't you read it? Rachel lent it to us weeks ago.

**Eddie** Is it good?

**Belinda** I don't know. I haven't had time to read it, have I?

**Neville** Can't tell you the last time I read a book.

**Belinda** I can. You read a quarter of one soft-porn novel shortly after we were married and that's your lot. We've been to the theatre twice and you fell asleep both times and we've been to one open-air jazz festival when we left early because it rained.

**Neville** We've been to the cinema.

**Belinda** Oh yes, I beg your pardon. I mustn't forget that visit.

**Neville** Nothing's ever on.

**Eddie** We don't go out much. We used to go to the disco. But now with the kids . . .

**Neville** (*winking*) You make your own amusements, don't you?

**Belinda** (*laughing mirthlessly*) Ho, ho, ho, ho, ho.

**Neville** Look, look, let me show you this. Watch this. (*He nudges Eddie and stands back*) Let there be lights.

*Neville presses the button on this control unit whilst pointing it at the Christmas tree. The lights come on. Belinda, on her ladder, wobbles and cries out*

**Belinda** Neville, would you not do that.

**Neville** (*laughing*) You like that?

**Eddie** Very clever.

**Belinda** I don't see the point of it. There's a switch on the wall.

**Neville** Save you bending down.

**Eddie** You build that yourself?

**Neville** Yes. Nothing much. Transmitter and a couple of relays. Nothing much. Watch this. And music, maestro.

*Neville presses the other button. This triggers off a cassette recorder concealed in the tub at the base of the tree. A loud children's Christmas song blares out*

**Belinda** (*screaming*) Neville!

**Neville** (*switching it off*) Sorry.

**Belinda** The kids are asleep up there.

**Neville** All right.

**Harvey** I say, I appear to have lost my film in here. I'm on another channel.

**Neville** Are you?

**Harvey** I've got the Russian ballet or something instead.

**Neville** It shouldn't have done that. That's funny.

**Belinda** Brilliant.

**Neville** I don't know how that happened.

*Neville goes into the sitting-room and disappears while he readjusts the set*

**Harvey** Just getting to the big chase. I don't want all this prancing about.
**Eddie** It must have crossed the signal.

*Neville reappears*

**Neville** That's a mystery, that is. Very interesting. (*He stands in the sitting-room doorway and presses the button again. The music blares out*)
**Belinda** Neville, for the last time . . .!
**Neville** (*switching it off*) Sorry. Just checking.
**Belinda** No, I mean seriously, what is the point of that? It's very clever but what's the point of it?
**Neville** It's for the kids.
**Belinda** For the kids? You're going to give that to a six-year-old and a four-year-old?
**Neville** They'll love it. They press this button and the lights go on. (*About to demonstrate*) You press this other button and . . .
**Belinda** (*interrupting him before he can demonstrate again*) Yes, all right. It's going to be terrific, isn't it? All Boxing Day, that thing switching on and off and driving us mad.
**Neville** I can turn down the volume.
**Belinda** Well, please wrap it up now and save it till Boxing Day.
**Neville** Sure.
**Belinda** It'll be a five minute wonder like everything else. (*Indicating a decoration*) Hand me that, will you?
**Neville** This? (*He passes it to her*)
**Eddie** I went in this morning to get Gary this truck he wanted. It cost a fortune. And when I tested it this evening, it was totally duff. I should've known. Everything I buy for them seems to be duff.
**Neville** I'll take a look at it if you like.
**Eddie** Oh, thanks. I didn't . . . Thanks.

*Pattie appears at the top of the stairs. She stands staring at Eddie*

(*Seeing her*) Oh hallo.
**Pattie** (*grimly*) You coming or not?

*Eddie wearily puts down his glass and starts up the stairs quite slowly. Pattie waits for him on the landing*

He won't go to sleep till he sees you. He's convinced himself now that you're dead.
**Eddie** Oh, great. Perhaps if you got a little firm with him occasionally it might help.
**Pattie** (*softly*) If I what?
**Eddie** I said if you got a little . . .
**Pattie** If I what?
**Eddie** You heard.
**Pattie** If I got a little what? Firm? Did you say firm, by any chance? Don't try to be funny. Please.

*Pattie comes down the stairs, leaving Eddie standing half-way to the top looking a trifle embarrassed. He is unsure as to how much has been heard of this quiet little exchange. Eventually he braves it out, smiles, shrugs and goes on upstairs*

*Eddie goes off*

**Belinda** You know, I'm a bit worried. This man might be on that eight-oh-five. I think someone ought to meet him. I mean, he could just be stranded there. Somebody ought to meet him.

**Neville** I wouldn't know him from Adam.

**Pattie** (*muttering, almost inaudibly*) He'll have to deal with Gary. I can cope with the girls but I can't handle Gary when he's like that . . .

**Belinda** Give Pattie a drink.

**Neville** I'm going to. Pattie, would you like a drink?

**Pattie** Er—yes, I'll—er . . .

*Bernard enters swiftly from the kitchen*

**Bernard** Er . . .

**Belinda** Bernard.

**Bernard** The first-aid kit is—where?

**Belinda** (*promptly*) The first-aid kit is in the third drawer down to the left of the stove in a big white tin.

**Bernard** Right. (*He turns to go*)

**Belinda** Bernard, what's happened?

**Bernard** Oh, she just . . . The edges of those saucepans of yours are pretty sharp. Quite dangerous.

*Bernard goes*

**Belinda** I've never cut myself on them.

**Neville** This lamb's going to be very pink, isn't it?

*Neville follows Bernard off to the kitchen*

**Pattie** No, I don't think I'll have a drink now. I'll wait. I've just been reading them that Wendy House book, you know.

**Belinda** Oh, no, you mean the—(*saying this very fast*)—Weird and Wonderful World of the Wackety Witch's Wendy House.

**Pattie** Yes. I couldn't understand it. It's all sort of nonsense really, isn't it? They seem to like it.

**Belinda** Yes, well. They like nonsense, don't they?

**Pattie** Funny book to sit down and write though. For a living.

**Belinda** Could you pass me that? By your foot.

**Pattie** This?

**Belinda** Ta.

**Harvey** Bel, you're the one who's mad about sheepdogs, aren't you?

**Belinda** Oh, lovely, yes. Adore them.

**Harvey** This one's a real beauty. You should see this one.

**Belinda** Oh, super, yes. I remember him. (*She continues with her tree, having not moved*)

*Rachel, comes clumping downstairs, a little red-eyed*

Oh, Rachel. Look, I was saying, I think you ought to meet the eight-oh-five. I mean, supposing he gets here and there's no . . .

**Rachel** It's really of no interest to me whatsoever.

*Rachel goes into the sitting-room and plonks herself on the window-seat. Belinda pulls a face to Pattie*

**Harvey** Ah, Rachel. You're back.

**Rachel** Yes.

**Harvey** Has he come? This chap of yours?

**Rachel** No.

*Rachel sits staring into space*

**Belinda** How's the baby?

**Pattie** (*listlessly*) Oh, coming along.

*Belinda steps back to pick up her drink*

**Harvey** Cutting it a bit fine, isn't he?

**Rachel** How do you mean?

**Harvey** Well, he's going to miss his dinner in a minute, isn't he?

**Rachel** It's nothing whatever to do with me.

**Harvey** Oh. Mind you, since it's Phyllis cooking it, that may be to his advantage. I've never known anybody cook lamb like she does. Should be punishable by law.

*Belinda sips her drink whilst admiring her handiwork*

*Bernard hurries through from the kitchen. He goes into the dining-room and begins to take the knives and forks out of the drawer in the sideboard. He begins to sort out the cutlery into piles: nine in each, on top of the sideboard*

**Pattie** No, the thing is, I don't really want to have this baby, you know.

**Belinda** Why not?

**Pattie** I don't know.

**Belinda** Four's too many perhaps?

**Pattie** Three, four, what's the difference?

**Belinda** (*shrugging*) Well.

**Pattie** I think maybe it's because I know that Eddie doesn't really want it.

**Belinda** Oh.

**Pattie** I mean, I think he feels we just get in his way half the time.

**Belinda** He does?

**Pattie** He hasn't said so but I get that feeling.

**Belinda** What are you supposed to be getting in the way off?

**Pattie** You know, his career and all that. I think he feels he could have done a lot better.

**Belinda** Darling, Eddie would have done a lot better if he hadn't had grand ideas about starting up on his own. He should never have left Neville, you know that.

**Pattie** I know, I know.

**Belinda** He was an idiot.

**Pattie** I know he's an idiot. I've told him he was an idiot.
**Belinda** So. It's no use him blaming you and the kids.
**Pattie** He won't be told though. He's an idiot. It's amazing him and Nev are still friends.
**Belinda** Oh well. You'll never break that up.
**Harvey** Now, the chap I'd really like to meet is the chap who wrote this.
**Rachel** What?
**Harvey** This film. I'd like to meet the writer of this film. He must have a hell of an imagination.
**Rachel** Oh. You think somebody actually wrote this?
**Harvey** Of course somebody wrote it.
**Rachel** Oh, you amaze me.
**Harvey** What a damned stupid thing to say. How utterly damned stupid. They'd hardly make it up as they went along, would they? They'd hardly invent the dialogue, would they?
**Rachel** I don't know what dialogue you mean. Nobody's said anything for ten minutes. Nobody's talking at all.
**Harvey** Well, of course, they're not talking. Not at the moment. They're punching each other.
**Rachel** Oh yes.
**Harvey** They can't talk while they're fighting, can they?
**Rachel** No. True.
**Harvey** Damn stupid thing to say then, wasn't it? Oh now, this is good. This bit's marvellous. You watch this fellow on the left.

*During the above, Pattie drifts towards the sitting-room doorway*

**Pattie** What are they watching in here?
**Belinda** Oh, you know. The one they always have on. That one.
**Bernard** (*coming to the dining-room doorway clasping a handful of knives and forks*) Look—er—I'm sorry about earlier. I got heated. I'm sorry, that's all. (*He goes back into the dining-room and starts laying the table*)
**Belinda** That's OK, Bernard.
**Pattie** What's he talking about?
**Belinda** Nothing important.
**Pattie** I hope he's not planning another of his puppet shows.
**Belinda** He is.
**Pattie** Oh no.

*Rachel gets up abruptly from the window-seat, apparently having come to a decision. She pushes past Pattie who is still standing in the sitting-room doorway half watching the film*

**Rachel** Excuse me.

*Rachel goes to the coat-stand and starts to put on her coat and scarf again. Pattie hereafter becomes more and more drawn into the film in the sitting-room. During the following, she gradually moves into the room and finally sits where Rachel had been on the window-seat*

**Pattie** Oh yes, I remember this. It was great.

**Harvey** Marvellous.

*Belinda is apparently still absorbed in her tree decoration*

**Belinda** You're going to try the eight-oh-five, are you?
**Rachel** Well. I wouldn't want him stranded. It's totally unlikely he'll be on it. He'd have rung or something. He always rings. Except when he forgets, of course. He's always losing things. Pens, gloves, handkerchiefs. Never has a handkerchief. I mean, it doesn't matter a damn either way. It's just, it makes me look a bit of a—a bit stupid.
**Belinda** Not at all.
**Rachel** Still.

*Rachel stands in the front doorway shifting from foot to foot*

*Bernard goes through from the dining-room, back to the kitchen*

(*When Bernard's gone*) Thirty-eight-year-old woman behaving like a teenager, aren't I? Well, if he's not on this train, bugger him, that's what I say.
**Belinda** Good luck.
**Rachel** Yes.

*Rachel goes out the front door*

*A cry from Pattie and Harvey in unison*

**Harvey** Ha-ha!
**Pattie** Oooh! Terrific!

*Neville enters with three open bottles of claret*

**Neville** According to Joan of Arc out there, dinner will be in about ten minutes.
**Belinda** Is she winning?
**Neville** Possibly. But I have to say the leg of lamb is certainly looking the fresher of the two at present. I thought we might try this stuff tonight. The man who was standing in for the regular man at the off-licence that I don't normally go to was fully prepared to stake his reputation on it. So we could be on to a good thing.
**Belinda** (*gazing about the hall*) It's nice this, for the kids, isn't it?
**Neville** Kids?
**Belinda** Yes.
**Neville** What about them? They're not having any of this. (*He begins to ferret around in the sideboard for the wineglasses*)
**Belinda** (*in the dining-room doorway*) No, I mean when I went up to say good-night to our two earlier, they were so excited. Katie was anyway. I remembered feeling like that. I was so excited I just trembled. All these surprises all over the house, waiting. It was a really good time, wasn't it?
**Neville** I suppose so.
**Belinda** You must have been excited at Christmas, don't you remember?
**Neville** I remember Phyllis crying all night in the room next door.
**Belinda** Crying?

**Neville** Yes. She was terrified in case Father Christmas got into her room. Can you imagine that? Only happen to Phyllis. Santaphobia.

**Belinda** I don't even get any surprises these days. I know what I've got. I went out and bought them myself. I brought them home and wrapped them up. I even paid for them out of the joint account.

**Neville** Oh, come on.

**Belinda** You could at least have written the labels, Nev.

**Neville** Darling, it is Christmas time.

**Belinda** Happy Christmas, Belinda or something. To my dear wife, whose face seems faintly familiar or something . . .

**Neville** It is Christmas time.

**Belinda** That's what I'm saying.

**Neville** I don't have to tell you about Christmas time, do I?

**Belinda** No. You don't have to tell me about Christmas time.

**Neville** Like it or not, darling, you married a retailer. But if you would like me to tell you about Christmas time . . .

**Belinda** (*over this*) Oh dear God, he is now going to tell me about Christmas time . . .

**Neville** Because if you would——

**Belinda** Forget it.

**Neville** —I'd be quite happy . . .

**Belinda** Thank you.

**Neville** Just say the word.

**Belinda** Shut up.

*Belinda wanders back to the tree*

*Bernard hurries on from the kitchen with a covered dish*

**Bernard** First course coming up.

**Neville** Anyway, I hope I like whatever it is you've bought you.

**Belinda** You'll loathe it, I guarantee.

**Neville** Oh, good show.

*Neville puts the wine and glasses on the table. Bernard dumps the covered dish up the far end of the table and starts back for the kitchen*

**Belinda** That's the least I could do. (*As Bernard passes through the hall*) Do I take it, it's all ready, Bernard?

**Bernard** Yes. Phyllis is coming through shortly. She says can everyone please sit down. She's just preparing the gravy.

*Bernard hurries out*

**Belinda** (*going to the sitting-room door*) Did you hear that, folks? Food is on the table.

**Harvey** Just a minute, just a minute. This is a fight to the death.

**Belinda** Oh yes, I remember this bit.

**Pattie** Go on, get him.

*Eddie comes downstairs*

*Belinda stays in the sitting-room doorway*

**Eddie** (*to Belinda*) He'll do anything to stay awake, that Gary. Little monkey, you have to laugh.

*Bernard hurries back through to the dining-room with a stack of plates and disappears to the unseen part of the room*

**Bernard** Come on, everybody, it's on the table.
**Eddie** Oh, is it on the table? Right. (*Moving to the sitting-room door*) It's on the table apparently.
**Belinda** Just a sec. It's a good bit this.
**Eddie** Oh yes, that's right. This is the bit with the waterfall.
**Belinda** Yes.

*Bernard, having placed the stack of plates up the far end of the table with the covered dish, returns to the visible part of the dining-room*

*Neville finishes putting out the glasses*

**Neville** Well, I'm hungry anyway.
**Bernard** (*to Neville*) Could you hurry them in, Nev, it'll get cold?
**Neville** Where are they, anyway?

*Neville goes into the hall. Bernard busies himself around the dining-table, distributing paper table-napkins which he gets from the sideboard*

(*Seeing Eddie and Belinda in the doorway*) Come on, you lot.

*Harvey and Pattie, heeding the call, rise from their seats and start to back away very slowly from the set, reluctant to take their eyes from it. They join Belinda and Eddie in the sitting-room doorway*

**Neville** (*craning to see through them*) What are you all watching?
**Belinda** (*making room for him slightly*) Look.
**Neville** Oh, this thing. It's not on again, is it?
**Pattie** Ooh.
**Eddie** Whoops.
**Harvey** Ha-ha . . .
**Neville** Look out.
**Belinda** There he goes.
**Harvey** Not quite.

*Bernard comes back to the dining-room doorway*

**Bernard** What are you all doing? Come on.
**Belinda** Sorry, Bernard, coming. (*Back to the television*) Oh no.
**Bernard** (*joining them*) What are you all . . . (*Seeing the screen*) Oh good gracious. He's going to fall off that, isn't he?
**All** Shhh.

*Phyllis enters along the kitchen passageway, a woman in her late thirties. She is a woman exhausted and slightly drunk: a martyr to cooking. She totters into the hall*

**Neville** He's going.
**Pattie** There he goes.

**Harvey** He's gone. Bravo. (*He claps*)

*They all join in. Phyllis, arriving at this precise moment, assumes their applause is for her and acknowledges it with a modest curtsy*

**Phyllis** Thank you, thank you. (*Realizing her mistake*) Oh.
**Bernard** (*applauding her*) Well done, Phyllis, well done.
**Belinda** Oh, yes, well done, Phyllis. God, I'm starving.

*There is a general move towards the dining-room*

**Harvey** Tremendous entertainment.
**Pattie** I wish I'd seen it all now, really.

*Phyllis goes into the dining-room. Bernard stands in the doorway waving people through. General chatter*

**Bernard** (*over this*) Are we all coming?
**Harvey** All right, we're coming, we're coming. Don't rush us—we're coming.
**Bernard** It'll be cold.
**Phyllis** Yes, it'll be cold if you don't come now. It'll be cold.
**Bernard** Where's Rachel?
**Belinda** Gone to the station.
**Bernard** Oh dear, well, we can't wait, you know. We just can't wait.
**Belinda** No, you go on in, Bernard. I'm just coming, I promise.

*Bernard goes in to the dining-room, where people are now seating themselves. Practically, this means that Neville, Phyllis, Harvey and Eddie go offstage to the far end of the table. The chair at this end is left vacant for Belinda. The chair on her right is intended for Clive and is also left vacant. Next to him sits Pattie in view. To Belinda's left, is Bernard and on his left another vacant chair intended for Rachel. Belinda, meantime, looks into the sitting-room*

And why people can't switch things off when they've finished is totally beyond me . . . (*She switches off the television*)

*Belinda moves to the foot of the stairs and switches off the upper landing lights and also the hall overhead. This area now glows pleasantly, lit by just the Christmas tree lights and the glow of the table lamp. Belinda stands by the tree, still for a moment, in thought. She is about to join the dinner party when the front doorbell rings*

Oh.

*Clive, a man in his late twenties, appears in the doorway. He has a shy, pleasant manner. He wears an overcoat and holds a small suitcase*

**Clive** Mrs Bunker?
**Belinda** Oh, you're . . . Of course, you're—you're the novelist. Come in.
**Clive** (*stepping inside*) I'm sorry, the trains were extraordinary. It must be Christmas Eve . . .
**Belinda** That's quite all right. Let me take your . . .

*She starts to help him out of his coat*

It's cold.

**Clive** Oh yes.

**Belinda** I'm afraid Rachel's gone back to meet you.

**Clive** Oh Lord, that's awful. Do you think I ought to go back . . .?

**Belinda** (*hanging up his coat*) No, she's got the car. She won't be long. Come in, come in.

**Clive** Thank you. It's very good to meet you. I'm . . . (*He extends a hand*) How do you do? I'm Clive.

**Belinda** Belinda.

**Clive** Belinda.

**Belinda** Yes. (*They look at each other*) Hallo.

**Clive** Hallo.

**Belinda** Welcome.

**Clive** (*smiling*) Thank you.

*They stand by the tree, smiling at each other for a moment. Each looks rather good to the other: an effect enhanced only a little perhaps by the Christmas tree lights, as the Lights fade and—*

*the* CURTAIN *falls*

## SCENE 2

*The same. Christmas morning, around noon*

*Eddie in the dining-room is alone at the breakfast table. He is eating corn-flakes and reading a child's comic monster annual. New and shiny and straight from its paper bag. Whenever anyone enters the room, he makes as if to hide the book until he sees it is an adult, not a child. Around him on the table are the signs of one or two earlier breakfasters. In a second or so Belinda comes along the passage from the kitchen. She carries a tray and wears an apron. In contrast to the first scene, she is more practically dressed, as befits one back in domestic harness*

**Belinda** (*treading on something in the passageway*) Oh, these damn dolly mixtures are everywhere. They're everywhere. (*Examining her shoe*) Yuck. (*She continues on her way to the dining-room, hesitates and then looks into the sitting-room*)

*As Belinda turns back to the hall, Bernard comes downstairs, looking rather pale*

Good morning, Bernard, Happy Christmas.

**Bernard** Oh yes, Happy Christmas, Belinda.

**Belinda** I thought you'd be up earlier than this. You're usually around with the kids.

**Bernard** Well . . .

**Belinda** Bad night, was it?

**Bernard** Phyllis was up and down, up and down, I'm afraid.

**Belinda** Oh dear.

**Bernard** And if she's up and down, of course, then so am I.

**Belinda** Yes, well that's marriage for you.

**Bernard** She's off like a log now. I'm just going to fetch her a cup of coffee, if I may. Try and bring her to, gently. I think frankly, that yesterday was just a little bit too much for her. Frankly.

**Belinda** (*switching on the Christmas tree lights*) Yes, well she's done her bit now. She can just lie back and enjoy life, can't she? Coffee you wanted, didn't you? This should still be warm.

*She leads Bernard to the dining-room. Eddie jumps as she enters*

You still eating?

**Eddie** I'm just reading this. We got it for Gary. It's very good.

**Belinda** (*feeling the coffee-pot*) Yes, this seems OK. (*She finds a clean cup and pours some coffee*)

**Bernard** I thought I'd spend the rest of this morning unloading.

**Eddie** Unloading?

**Bernard** The puppet theatre.

**Eddie** Oh.

**Bernard** I've got it in the back of the estate. Just about. I can put it in the sitting-room, can I, Belinda? In a corner for now.
**Belinda** There's not too much of it, is there, Bernard?
**Bernard** Well, it'll tuck up quite small if I stack it.
**Belinda** Yes. She takes sugar, doesn't she? You'd better take that up as well. (*She hands him the sugar bowl*)
**Bernard** Thank you.
**Eddie** What's your show called this year, then, Bernard?
**Bernard** Er—*The Three Little Pigs.*
**Eddie** Ah.
**Belinda** Oh.
**Bernard** Bit of a change.
**Eddie** Just the three of them, is it?
**Bernard** What?
**Eddie** Pigs.
**Bernard** Yes.
**Eddie** Great.
**Bernard** Well, and their wives and families, of course.
**Eddie** Ah.

*Bernard goes out into the hall, carrying his cup and saucer and sugar bowl. Belinda clears the odd dirty cup on to her tray*

   *Pattie comes along the passage from the kitchen. She has on her hat, coat, scarf, gloves and boots*

**Pattie** (*calling back*) Wait there. No further than that. Not with your boots on.
**Bernard** (*as he goes up the stairs, to Pattie*) Good morning.
**Pattie** Good morning. What's all this on the floor?
**Bernard** Happy Christmas.

   *Bernard goes off upstairs*

**Pattie** Yes. (*Calling*) Eddie?
**Eddie** (*from the dining-room, without stirring*) Hallo.
**Pattie** (*back to the children*) Because my boots are clean. Because I haven't been jumping in drains, that's why. Now stay there, I won't be a minute. (*To the children*) I'm just fetching Daddy. Wait there. Now, wait, Zoë. Do you hear me?

*Belinda comes out of the dining-room with her tray loaded. She passes Pattie*

**Belinda** He's in there.
**Pattie** Right.

   *Belinda goes off to the kitchen*

**Pattie** (*entering the dining-room*) You still here?
**Eddie** Yes.
**Pattie** (*indicating his book*) You'll ruin that before he gets it.
**Eddie** It's good.

**Pattie** Are you coming then?
**Eddie** Coming?
**Pattie** For a walk. We're off for a walk.
**Eddie** Now?
**Pattie** Yes. Now.
**Eddie** I've only just got up.
**Pattie** That's not my fault. The kids have been up since six. So have I.
**Eddie** Then you go for a walk.
**Pattie** Look, you said last night you would.
**Eddie** Did I?
**Pattie** Oh Eddie, honestly, I've told them you're coming now.
**Eddie** Well, tell them I'm not.
**Pattie** You tell them. I'm not telling them. You tell them for once. You tell them you can't be bothered to go for a walk with them. You'd sooner sit reading comic books.
**Eddie** Pattie, just go for a walk if you're going. Go on. Leave me alone this morning, please.

*Pattie stares at him*

Go on.

**Pattie** (*snatching the book from the table*) And you can stop reading this as well. (*She tries to force it back into its paper bag but is unable to*)
**Eddie** Give it back.
**Pattie** It's supposed to be for Gary. It's not yours. I bought it for Gary.
**Eddie** Pattie, give it to me, please.
**Pattie** No, I'm wrapping it up for Gary.
**Eddie** Pattie, you will make me do something I will really regret in a minute. Now put the bloody book back on the table.
**Pattie** No.
**Eddie** Pattie, I'll—I really will—I shall do something—I really will—in a minute. I really will.
**Pattie** It won't be the first time, will it?
**Eddie** I really will.

*Belinda comes back from the kitchen and enters the dining-room*

**Belinda** (*feeling the atmosphere, briskly*) Yes, right.

*Belinda goes out again and back down the kitchen passageway*

*Pattie puts the book quietly back on the table and leaves the dining-room. She stands in the hall for a minute, staring fixedly at the Christmas tree, trying to compose herself*

*Bernard pads down the stairs. He has his gloves and jacket on*

**Bernard** (*as he passes Pattie*) Just going to start unloading.

*Pattie does not react*

*Bernard collects his hat from the hat-stand and goes out of the front door*

*Meanwhile Eddie reopens the book and stares at it, but it is doubtful whether at this moment he is reading it*

*Neville comes in from the kitchen with a tray of last night's knives and forks, now washed and ready to be put away*

**Neville** (*over his shoulder to the children as he comes through*) Mind your backs, small people. Don't crowd the doorway, please. (*To Pattie*) Excuse me, you're wanted.

**Pattie** (*turning*) What?

**Neville** There's a tiny deputation out here asking for you.

**Pattie** Oh yes.

*Pattie goes to the base of the tree and digging down retrieves a present, only half-wrapped with no more than a sheet of Christmas paper tucked round it. Neville meanwhile goes into the dining-room and deposits his tray on the sideboard*

**Neville** (*to Eddie*) And where were you at six-thirty, you swine?

**Eddie** Asleep.

**Neville** Yes. No-one else down yet?

**Eddie** No.

**Neville** Our author still in his attic?

**Eddie** I haven't seen him.

**Neville** They prefer them, you know. Authors. Attics.

**Eddie** Do they?

**Neville** So I read. But then they probably wrote it, didn't they? No Rachel either?

**Eddie** No.

**Neville** (*suggestively*) Ooo-ooo.

**Eddie** Oh. Are they . . .?

**Neville** I shouldn't think so.

**Eddie** No.

**Neville** Not with Rachel.

**Eddie** I can't imagine it. Do you think she does ever?

**Neville** Let's say not to my knowledge.

**Eddie** I can't imagine it.

**Neville** No.

*Pattie arrives and stands in the doorway holding the parcel*

Still I could be wrong. Look at Bernard and Phyllis.

**Eddie** Quite.

**Neville** Mind you, we've only their word for that, haven't we?

*They laugh. They see Pattie*

**Pattie** (*coolly*) Excuse me, please. (*She goes to the table and dumps her package down in front of Eddie*) Perhaps you'd like to look at this, please. It doesn't work. It didn't work when you bought it, and if you can't get it to work now, you'd better throw it away. Because if Gary opens it tomorrow and it doesn't work, it'll break his heart. All right?

**Eddie** Right.

**Pattie** I'll see you later then. (*She goes to the hall*)

**Neville** (*as she goes*) Morning.

*Pattie goes out to the kitchen*

*Eddie looks at Neville but says nothing*

Fancy a brisk walk to the village when they open?
**Eddie** You're on.
**Neville** Just a quick pint. Get out of their way.
**Eddie** Good idea.

*Eddie unwraps the present. It is a battery-operated vehicle, quite sophisticated, perhaps the type that is controlled by a remote lead. It is at present very inoperative. Eddie glares at it and shakes it, trying to get it to work*

**Neville** (*who is putting away the cutlery, pausing*) What have you got there?
**Eddie** Not working.
**Neville** Oh dear.
**Eddie** Nothing I buy ever does work. Four hundred of them on the shelves, three hundred and ninety-nine of them in perfect order and in I come. I'll have to take it back.

*Bernard enters through the front door*

**Neville** (*laying down his cutlery and coming to the table*) Let's have a look then.
**Eddie** Could be a loose connection, I suppose.
**Neville** Possibly, possibly. Easily find out, can't we? (*He examines it*) Yes . . . Batteries OK, are they?
**Eddie** Oh yes.

*They stare at it*

*Bernard makes the first of many journeys as he brings on first, his puppet theatre in pieces—a simple box framework with an operative curtain, all of which bolts together, then boxes of string puppets and finally small props and stacks of hand-painted cardboard scenery. Hours of love have gone into the creation of it all though it remains, sadly, rather inept. He stacks this in the corner of the sitting-room by the window-seat. On his way out, he stops at the dining-room door*

**Bernard** I'm just loading my stuff in there.
**Neville** Oh, yes.
**Bernard** For my play. I won't disturb you.
**Neville** Right.
**Bernard** *The Three Little Pigs.*
**Neville** Oh, yes. Just the three of them, is it? (*He laughs*)
**Bernard** (*very shortly for him*) Yes.

*Bernard goes out for the next load*

**Neville** It just occurred to me, Eddie. Something for you to ponder.
**Eddie** What's that?
**Neville** Now, I know you left the firm for good reasons. You wanted to

start on your own and good luck—nobody minded and we've stayed
friends through it all but let's be honest, Eddie, things haven't worked
out, have they?

**Eddie** Well . . .

**Neville** So. Now, this is between us. No-one else. All right? We're going
to open a third branch, all right?

**Eddie** Another?

**Neville** Yes.

**Eddie** Where?

**Neville** Shall we say not twenty miles south of here.

**Eddie** South? Oh, you mean . . .

**Neville** Right.

**Eddie** Where?

**Neville** Main street, OK? Boots the Chemist here on the corner before it
moved, right?

**Eddie** Yes.

**Neville** Then there's the dry cleaners here and the delicatessen on the
other corner. Do you get me?

**Eddie** By the . . .

**Neville** Yes.

**Eddie** On the other side of . . .

**Neville** Yes, that's it. You've got it, you've got it.

**Eddie** How did you get that?

**Neville** Signed yesterday.

**Eddie** They were all after that.

**Neville** I know. Still, as I say, we shall very shortly be needing a third
manager and a full staff. Need I say more?

**Eddie** Well.

**Neville** Just think about it. Over the festivities. I must know by the New
Year. All right.

**Eddie** (*overwhelmed*) Yes, yes . . .

**Neville** (*rising and taking the toy with him*) I'm just going to put this on
the bench. Check it over. Won't be a second.

**Eddie** (*still rather bewildered*) Right. You don't need to go to any . . .

**Neville** No, this is a challenge, this is. You know me, I like a challenge.

*Neville goes out through the hall and along the passageway, where,
momentarily, he glances at his feet as they tread through more dolly
mixture. He then goes off with the toy. As he does so, Bernard returns
through the front door with a second load. He goes into the sitting-room*

**Bernard** (*to Neville*) Load number two.

*Bernard leaves and goes out of the front door. Belinda meanwhile comes
back along the hall passageway armed with a damp cloth*

**Belinda** These damned sweets. (*She stoops and scrubs at the floor*) Why
they can't put them in their ugly little mouths. Instead of all over my
floor . . . (*Looking up*) And Bernard—(*she marches to the front door*)—
will you not leave this front door open, please? We have the central

heating on at full blast. Thank you. (*She heaves an impatient sigh. She is spoiling for trouble. Through the dining-room doorway, she sees the cutlery on the sideboard only half put away. She marches in and confronts Eddie*) Has he just left this?

**Eddie** (*looking up from his book, startled*) Uh?

**Belinda** This cutlery. Has he just left this half done and walked away?

**Eddie** Yes, I think he's just . . .

**Belinda** (*turning and shouting out into the hall*) Neville, have you just left this half done? God damn it, why can't he do one thing? One little tiny thing to help! That's all I've asked him to do the entire holiday.

**Eddie** (*rising alarmed*) Look, it's OK, I'll . . .

**Belinda** (*fiercely*) No. No. Sit down. You leave everything exactly there as it is. You are not to touch a thing. Do you hear me?

**Eddie** (*sitting again*) Yes. No, no . . .

**Belinda** That is Neville's job. That is Neville's single, solitary job for the whole holiday period. That is Neville's job for Christmas Eve, Christmas Day, Boxing Day, right through until New Year's Day. That's all Neville has to do. That. Just put away a few knives and forks. And he is bloody well going to do it.

**Eddie** (*awed by this outburst*) Yes. OK.

*Belinda sweeps out of the dining-room*

*Clive comes downstairs during this, understandably rather cautiously. He carries two wrapped parcels: one that looks like a box of chocolates, the other definitely a bottle*

*Belinda sees him. Her manner mellows appreciably*

**Belinda** Oh, good morning.

**Clive** Morning. Happy Christmas.

**Belinda** Happy Christmas to you, yes. You must be ready for breakfast.

**Clive** Oh no. No, really, thank you, no. I'm still rather full of lamb, actually.

**Belinda** Yes, it was filling. It's the way Phyllis does it. Coffee then, you'd like coffee? We usually have the main Christmas dinner about five so the kids can join us—it's a bit of a madhouse but . . .

**Clive** I wouldn't say no to that.

**Belinda** (*scurrying into the dining-room again*) Right. (*Snatching up the coffee-pot*) I'll make you some fresh. This'll be cold. Wait there.

**Clive** (*following her into the dining-room doorway*) Thanks. Please don't go to any . . .

**Belinda** Wait there.

*Belinda goes off to the kitchen*

*Clive sees Eddie. He indicates Belinda and laughs. Eddie does likewise*

**Eddie** Morning.

**Clive** Morning.

**Eddie** Write any more books during the night, did you?

**Clive** No, no. 'Fraid not.

**Eddie** Hey.

**Clive** Yes?

**Eddie** You want any tips, any ideas for books, you've come to the right place.

**Clive** Oh yes?

**Eddie** If you're stuck, come to me. I can give you some ideas.

**Clive** Right. I will. Thank you. (*He wanders back to the centre of the hall. He puts the presents that he is still holding down on the table*)

*Bernard enters with further equipment*

**Bernard** Oh, good morning. Merry Christmas.

**Clive** And to you.

**Bernard** I'm just unloading.

**Clive** Ah.

**Bernard** (*confidentially*) I do these little puppet shows, you know. Every year. For the children. A little treat. Nothing spectacular. I write them myself. Make all the bits and pieces.

**Clive** Oh, marvellous.

**Bernard** Not that I call myself a writer, not in the same bracket as yourself.

**Clive** (*encouragingly*) You never know, if you keep going.

**Bernard** I do it purely for love. I'd never dream of taking money for it.

**Clive** Ah.

*Harvey appears in the front doorway, returning from church in his dark coat, beret and gloves*

**Harvey** Good morning.

**Clive** Good morning.

**Bernard** (*seeing Harvey*) Excuse me. (*He goes into the sitting-room*)

**Harvey** Sunny but brisk.

**Clive** Really?

**Harvey** Have to keep moving. It's one of those days. Just been to church.

**Clive** Oh, have you?

**Harvey** Pay my respects, you know. I like to go once a year, that's all. Just in case. Keep the options open, eh? (*He laughs*)

*Clive laughs. Bernard squeezes between them on his way out*

**Bernard** Excuse me.

**Harvey** Good morning.

**Bernard** Good morning.

*Bernard goes out*

**Harvey** (*after Bernard has gone*) Want a tip?

**Clive** What's that?

**Harvey** If you're ever taken ill, struck down, catch a virus, have an accident, break a leg or something, you know. If anything ever happens to you in that line and you're in need of a doctor . . .

**Clive** Yes?

**Harvey** Then for Pete's sake, steer clear of him.

**Clive** Why?

**Harvey** He's the worst doctor in the world.

**Clive** Is he?

**Harvey** Total washout. He's sent people to their graves, convinced they
were critically ill when in fact they were perfectly fit. He's pronounced
people A-One, and they've dropped dead in his waiting-room on the
way out. Very poor doctor with a second-class brain. Don't go near
him, he's lethal. You've seen his wife?

**Clive** Phyllis?

**Harvey** My niece. See what he's done to her. She always was peculiar,
mind you. Now she's completely loopy. She drinks like a fish, too. He
ought to be struck off before he does any more damage.

*Bernard returns through the front door, with more stuff*

**Bernard** Excuse me, please.

**Harvey** What's all that?

**Bernard** Just my theatre.

**Harvey** Oh Gawd.

*Bernard goes into the sitting-room*

(*To Clive, confidentially*) Dozy little sod. Wait till he sees what I've got
him for Christmas.

**Clive** What's that?

**Harvey** Something to wake his ideas up. (*Removing his coat*) The biggest
alarm clock you've ever seen. Alarm like a fire bell. Got it second-hand.
Slightly faulty. Goes off without the slightest warning. Always find
something. Last year I gave him a box of maroons. Set one off in his
bedroom. I ran back from church, would you believe that?

**Clive** Ran?

**Harvey** I still keep fit. Thirty-seven years with a security firm, you see.

**Clive** Were you?

**Harvey** Fighting the bastards on the streets most of the time. Clubs,
ammonia, pick-axe handles, pepper, socks full of sand . . .

**Bernard** (*squeezing past them again*) Excuse me.

*Bernard goes out*

**Harvey** Not that you could ever stop it. Not on your own. It's an irre-
versible process. It's all coming apart, you know. The whole fabric.
Ripping like tissue paper. One day, we'll wake up—if we wake up at
all, that is—and our so-called civilization will have vanished overnight.
And you can put that in your book. Here, here—(*he invites Clive to
place a hand on his stomach*)—feel that? Go on, put your hand there.
What's that feel like? To you?

**Clive** Well . . .

**Harvey** That's sixty-five years old, that is, next year. Would you believe
that? I'm ready. You come up against me, matey, you'll come up against
that. (*He crashes his fist into his stomach—an impressive blow*)

**Clive** Heavens.

**Harvey** (*warming to his task*) Hey, hey. (*He beckons Clive over again*)

*Clive approaches cautiously as Harvey places a leg on the hall chair and pulls up his trouser as far as his knee. He reveals a throwing knife strapped in a sheath to the side of his leg*

What do you make of this? (*He pulls the knife from its sheath*)

*Clive retreats slightly*

That's a balanced, bone-handled, razor sharp throwing knife, that is. Six inches of Sheffield steel there. You give me trouble, I can have this out of its sheath, across the room and sticking between your shoulder-blades before you could turn round.

*Clive laughs nervously*

I'm ready.

**Clive** Yes, you look ready.

**Harvey** I've got a gun upstairs as well. Put six of those into you while I'm at it, eh? (*He laughs*)

**Clive** (*laughing too*) Yes, yes.

**Harvey** Put that in your book. (*He goes into the sitting-room*) My God, look at all this junk here. The man's mad. He's a complete lunatic. Now then. Twelve forty-eight. Just in time for *The Ape Man*, eh. (*He switches on the television and settles in his chair. Within a few moments, he falls gently asleep*)

*Bernard enters with more stuff*

**Bernard** (*whispering to Clive as he passes*) He's mad. Do steer clear of him, he's completely mad. He's almost certifiable really.

*Bernard goes into the sitting-room*

*Belinda comes along the passage with a cup of coffee*

**Belinda** I'm sorry I've been so long.

**Clive** That's all right.

**Belinda** (*turning into the dining-room*) I had to make some fresh. Now, where would you. . . (*She sees Eddie is still in there engrossed in his book and turns swiftly back to the hall*) Well, you can have it out here, can't you? I'll keep you company. The kitchen's a mess at the moment or I'd— You don't take sugar?

**Clive** No, thank you.

**Belinda** Fine. Please, sit down. (*She indicates the chair by the hall table, then sees Clive's presents sitting there*) Oh.

**Clive** Ah yes. For you. I forgot.

**Belinda** Thank you. How lovely. Surprises.

**Clive** It's just some Scotch and a box of chocolates.

**Belinda** Ah.

*Bernard comes out of the sitting-room, through the hall and out of the front door*

**Clive** Just to say thank you for looking after me.

**Belinda** (*taking them from him*) How lovely. All for me.

**Clive** Well, I thought one of them might be for your husband.

**Belinda** No, that's all right. I can manage both, that's fine.

*She puts them down at the base of the tree and sits on the bench. Clive sits at the table and sips his coffee. They look at each other. An embarrassed silence*

I can't work out whether I'm nervous of you because you're a writer or nervous of you because you're famous.

**Clive** Well, if it's any help, I'm not all that famous.

**Belinda** You're not?

**Clive** Well, I'm hardly a household name.

**Belinda** Oh, thank God. You know, I felt awful because I'd never heard of you. You see, the way Rachel went on I really thought I ought to have heard of you and I felt terribly guilty. Because I do try to keep up. I read all the bits in the Sundays and all that sort of thing but even that's terribly difficult. I mean, there's so many of you, aren't there? Names to watch, I mean. Every week there's another dozen. The most exciting since, the best since, the most promising since so-and-so and occasionally, it's really awful because I've never even heard of so-and-so. And at one time, honestly, I used to religiously note down all the names and try to learn them so that I'd recognize them when they cropped up again. But then half of them never did crop up again. And there I was. Stuck with a lot of useless names that nobody'd heard of. Like an out-of-date phone book. All the same, I think one really does have to try and make the effort. Take an interest. Don't you? Specially someone like me. Otherwise I feel I'd just—die really. (*She pauses, a little breathless*)

**Clive** Well, in the probable words of a Sunday paper, I'm clearly the funniest new novelist to have arrived this year and a welcome young face to the literary scene that we hope soon to hear more of. (*He rises*) My book which is entitled *Now Pull The Other One*, is at present number seventeen in the Best Seller list which is admittedly pretty good for hardback but could be better. Briefly, it's the story of a man who, at a tender age, plunges into marriage and kids and divorce and comes out the other side thinner but wiser. It has been described as painfully witty, or wittily painful, I forget which. But really and truly it was one of those books that got written as therapy when I sat down and tried to get the whole marriage out of my system. Which I have. And that makes me rather lucky really. Because a lot of people, during the course of their lives, need to do that. But very few of them expect to make a lot of money out of it like I have.

**Belinda** I see.

**Clive** So now you don't have to read it either. (*He is now quite close to her*)

**Belinda** Oh, I've started it. I've not got very far, I'm afraid. Well no, actually, I haven't got anywhere.

**Clive** Never mind. (*He smiles at her*)

*A silence*

*Bernard comes through with some more stuff. He goes into the sitting-room*

*Belinda rises. They are close together*

**Belinda** Well. (*She laughs*)

**Clive** (*laughing*) Yes.

**Belinda** If you'll excuse me, I'd better put away all those noons and sporks. (*She smiles at her mistake*) Rather knives and sporks. (*She pauses, confused*) I don't know why I'm being quite so stupid just because you're a writer. I'm not normally like this, I'm sorry. I'm usually much more interesting, honestly.

**Clive** Perhaps you should stop thinking of me as a writer. Think of me as just an ordinary, normal, common or garden, basic man. Does that help?

**Belinda** Er—no. Frankly. No . . .

**Clive** Oh. Sorry.

**Belinda** Don't be sorry.

*They look at each other again*

*Rachel appears on the stairs*

*Clive sees her first*

**Clive** Oh, hallo.

**Rachel** Hallo.

**Belinda** Hallo.

**Rachel** Hallo.

**Belinda** Happy Christmas.

**Rachel** What are you doing out here?

**Clive** Just having coffee.

**Rachel** Odd place to have coffee, isn't it? In the hall.

**Belinda** Oh, I don't know . . . Finished?

**Clive** (*handing her his cup*) Thank you.

*Bernard passes through and goes out by the front door*

**Belinda** I must get on.

**Rachel** Are we going out then?

**Clive** Oh yes.

**Rachel** I told you you'd regret it in the morning. Making rash promises after large meals.

**Belinda** It's lovely out. Sunny but a bit chilly.

*Belinda goes off along the kitchen passageway*

*Rachel comes downstairs*

**Rachel** I thought I'd take you through the farm. Do you mind farms?

**Clive** No.

**Rachel** I love visiting the cows. I adore cows, don't you? Actually I prefer them to horses. Then I thought, if you liked, we could walk down as far as the village—might even have a drink if you fancied it—

and then back round the other way along the river. It's not as far as
it sounds.

**Clive** Lovely.

**Rachel** Did you sleep?

**Clive** Wonderfully.

**Rachel** You look a bit shattered. We did what we could with that attic
but I'm afraid it's still an attic. You were warm enough?

**Clive** Very.

**Rachel** Oh, good. They were a bit short of bedding. I lugged some of my
stuff down from the flat. Oh look. I have to ask you. I promised I
would. You can say no. Would you be Father Christmas this year? On
Boxing Day? For the kids. We always try to get someone they're least
likely to recognize, though they always do. You can easily say no if you
hate the idea.

**Clive** No. It's something I've always desperately wanted to do.

**Rachel** Visitor's chore, I'm afraid. All right. Well, let's go, shall we?
Coats.

**Clive** Lead on.

**Rachel** Are those your only shoes?

**Clive** Oh. Yes.

**Rachel** Hell. Hang on, I think they have boots upstairs. In fact, I know
they do. Wait there. (*She starts upstairs*) You sure you're all right?

**Clive** Yes, of course.

**Rachel** (*looking at him thoughtfully*) Yes. I have a feeling I should have
got up a bit earlier this morning for some reason.

**Clive** What do you mean?

**Rachel** Don't go away.

*Clive smiles*

  *Rachel goes off upstairs*

  *Bernard passes through again with more stuff*

**Bernard** Nearly there.

**Clive** Good.

*Bernard goes into the sitting-room*

  *Belinda comes back from the kitchen. She carries a scarf in one hand and
  boots in the other*

**Belinda** Look, I was just thinking. If you're going for walks around here,
you'll need boots.

**Clive** Oh, I think Rachel's . . .

**Belinda** Here.

**Clive** Rachel's just getting me some.

**Belinda** Rachel?

**Clive** She went to fetch some upstairs.

**Belinda** There's none up there. Have these. They're Nev's. They should
fit.

**Clive** (*sitting and trying them on*) Thanks.

*Bernard goes out again through the front door*

**Belinda** And I brought you a scarf in case you haven't got one. It's mine so please don't lose it.

**Clive** Thank you.

*Rachel appears at the top of the stairs with some boots*

**Rachel** There. I knew there were some in the attic. I saw them when we were . . . (*she registers Clive*). Oh.

**Belinda** I've just lent him Nev's.

**Clive** Sorry.

**Rachel** Oh. Well. Wasted journey, wasn't it? (*She drops the boots over the banisters*)

**Belinda** God knows whose those are. Probably belonged to the builders. I'll take them out the back.

*Clive stands up. Rachel comes downstairs*

Are those OK for you?

**Clive** They're fine. Perfect fit.

**Rachel** (*pulling on her coat*) Off we go then.

**Clive** (*following her*) OK.

**Belinda** Oh wait. Here. (*She holds out her scarf*)

**Clive** Ah. (*He goes to take it*)

**Rachel** What's that?

**Belinda** It's a scarf for Clive.

**Rachel** He doesn't need a scarf.

**Belinda** Yes, he does. It's cold.

**Rachel** That's your scarf.

**Belinda** Yes, I know it is but I'm not going out, am I?

**Rachel** He can't wear that.

**Belinda** Why not?

**Rachel** It's a woman's scarf. He can't wear a woman's scarf.

**Belinda** It's not a woman's scarf. It's just a scarf.

**Rachel** He'd look extraordinary.

**Belinda** Oh Rachel, don't be idiotic.

**Rachel** I'm not being idiotic. I just refuse to be seen going out with a man dressed in a woman's scarf. I'm sorry.

**Belinda** Rachel, for God's sake.

**Clive** It's all right, really. I don't need a scarf. I've gone off the whole idea of a scarf. Thanks all the same.

**Belinda** OK. Suit yourself.

**Rachel** (*irritably, thrusting Clive's coat at him*) Oh, do come on, if you're coming.

*Rachel goes out by the front door*

**Clive** Goodbye, then.

**Belinda** Goodbye. I'll see you later.

**Clive** Yes.

**Belinda** Keep warm, won't you?
**Clive** I will.

*Clive goes out the front door after Rachel*

*Belinda picks up the scarf and the boots Rachel has discarded and is about to head for the kitchen*

*Neville comes along the passage, still with the toy vehicle. He is fiddling with it. It now works occasionally when he jabs at it with a screwdriver*

**Belinda** What are you doing?
**Neville** Trying to fix this.
**Belinda** What is it?
**Neville** Eddie's present for Gary. You see, they've actually wired it so that it shorts out every time you switch on. That's disgraceful. Where are you off to?
**Belinda** Nowhere.
**Neville** You look like you're going out.
**Belinda** Afraid not. Not able to.
**Neville** We might pop out in a minute. Eddie and me. For a pint.
**Belinda** Thought you might.
**Neville** Well. (*He sits and continues with his task*)
**Belinda** (*tentatively*) Nev . . .
**Neville** (*still absorbed*) Um?

*Throughout the following, Neville stays totally absorbed*

**Belinda** Nev?
**Neville** Mm?
**Belinda** I'd say on the whole, we'd stayed a very happy couple, wouldn't you?
**Neville** Oh yes.
**Belinda** When you look at some of our friends.
**Neville** Mm.
**Belinda** I mean, I know we have rows but all the same, I don't know anybody who seems to be happier than us. Of our age. Younger couples sometimes. Not always. I mean, I think we could both say without any false modesty that we're still very much in love, wouldn't you? (*A slight pause*) I would.
**Neville** Mm.
**Belinda** I know it's a difficult thing to define. Love. Obviously it's not like it used to be but then who'd expect that after—eight and a half years. Perhaps we're not so passionate. But we're still in love.
**Neville** Mm?
**Belinda** Aren't we?
**Neville** Yes.
**Belinda** I think there are definitely other things more important, more lasting than passion. Companionship and sharing the same jokes. And familiarity.
**Neville** Sure.

**Belinda** I mean, maybe love's too strong a word to use. Perhaps it's friendship I'm talking about. We're still friends. That's what I mean.

**Neville** True.

**Belinda** And there really can be friendship between a man and a woman. Maybe not friends like you and, say, Eddie or between me and some—woman friend. I don't think a man and a woman could ever get that close. No. Not as friends.

**Neville** No.

**Belinda** But we still definitely have something, don't we? Apart from sharing the same house. And the same children. We must have.

**Neville** (*after a pause*) Yes, I'd say that was—very true, yes.

**Belinda** What is?

**Neville** What you said. (*He rises*) Look, I'd better go and get that drink in. You be all right, will you?

**Belinda** Yes—yes . . .

**Neville** (*ruffling her hair*) Cheer up, then. Love me?

**Belinda** Yes.

**Neville** That's what I like to hear. (*Calling*) Eddie, we're off. You fit?

**Eddie** (*springing up*) OK.

**Neville** I think I've traced the fault on this. (*He moves off towards the kitchen*)

**Eddie** Oh, terrific. (*To Belinda, following Neville off*) We're just going to the pub.

*Neville goes off*

**Belinda** (*savagely*) Oh super, super.

*Eddie, rather puzzled, goes off after Neville*

*Belinda stands, still holding on to her scarf and boots, desolate*

*Bernard enters with more stuff*

**Bernard** That's the lot. All unloaded.

**Belinda** Ah.

**Bernard** (*holding up a puppet to show her*) Look, see. The Big Bad Wolf. See. (*Making wolf noises*) Grrr. Wrrr.

**Belinda** (*smiling faintly*) Oh, yes . . .

**Bernard** Better be careful or he'll huff and he'll puff and he'll blow your house down, eh? (*He laughs and goes into the sitting-room*)

*Belinda, in a moment, wanders thoughtfully back to the kitchen, as the Lights fade and—*

*the* CURTAIN *falls*

## SCENE 3

*The same. Late Christmas evening, around midnight*

*The house party have wined and dined, particularly wined and there is an air of weary merriment about the place generally. In the dining-room, playing a game of Snakes and Ladders, another present for the children, are Neville, Phyllis, Clive and Bernard. All, especially Phyllis, are noisier than usual. Bernard keeps giving his wife apprehensive glances. In the darkened sitting-room, asleep in the armchair, paper hat on head, mouth wide open is Eddie. Sitting on the window-seat clasping the remainder of her drink, alone and still, is Rachel. At the start of the action, Phyllis is just having her turn at the game. It is all very drunk and hysterical*

**Phyllis** (*the others counting with her*) Three, four, five, six. I've missed it, I've missed the snake.
**Neville** Lucky, lucky.
**Clive** You missed the ladder too.
**Neville** Bernard's turn.
**Bernard** (*unhappily*) Oh, no, it's not my turn again.
**Phyllis** Yes, it is.
**Neville** Go on.
**Bernard** Oh, I'm not enjoying this. It's really . . .
**Phyllis** Go on, Bernard. Shake the dice. For heaven's sake.
**Bernard** (*doing so*) Oh.
**Clive** Is he going to do it again?
**Neville** Five, five, get a five.

*Bernard releases the dice*

**Phyllis** He has!
**Bernard** One, two . . .
**Neville** He's done it again.
**Clive** Go on, three, four . . .
**Bernard** I can't have done it again.
**Phyllis** Five! And down he goes.
**Bernard** Oh, this is ridiculous.

*Pattie enters from the kitchen and looks round the hall. She has on an apron over her dress and carries a tray*

**Neville** That's what? Eight times that's happened to Bernard. That's unbelievable.
**Bernard** It always happens to me.
**Neville** I mean, what are the chances if you were calculating the odds . . .
**Phyllis** He never wins anything.
**Clive** Astronomic.

**Neville** That's a good word. Astronomic. See we've got a writer.

*Pattie comes into the dining-room*

**Bernard** Well, I've finished. That's the end of me.

**Neville** Shame.

**Bernard** (*to Phyllis*) I'm going to get the bottles now, dear.

**Neville** Bottles? Get one for me, will you?

**Bernard** (*rising*) No, no. Hot-water-bottles.

**Phyllis** (*screaming with laughter*) Get one for me! (*Nudging Clive*) I thought he meant bottles, too.

**Clive** Yes.

*Pattie starts clearing the table of coffee cups and used glasses*

**Pattie** These cups finished with?

**Phyllis** Yes, they're finished with. Whose turn?

**Clive** Mine.

**Neville** Clive's turn.

**Clive** (*preparing to shake the dice*) Now then, six, six, six.

**Neville** (*to Pattie*) Does she want a hand out there?

**Pattie** No, we've done it all now. Too late.

**Bernard** I'm fetching the bottles now.

**Neville** We'd have lent a hand. She didn't have to do it all.

**Pattie** Too late.

**Bernard** I'm fetching the bottles now, dear.

**Phyllis** Well, I'm afraid I'm not doing a thing. Not this evening.

**Bernard** Quite right, quite right.

**Phyllis** I did everything last night. It's somebody else's turn.

**Pattie** You didn't clear up last night because I did.

**Phyllis** And who cooked it, child? Who cooked that lovely lamb you were eating?

**Bernard** All right, dear, all right.

**Neville** Are we playing or not?

**Pattie** I'm not saying you didn't. All I'm saying . . .

**Bernard** (*relieving her of her tray*) I'll take those out, Pattie. I'll take those out.

**Pattie** Thank you.

*Bernard hurries out and along to the kitchen*

**Clive** Right, I'm having my turn. (*He shakes the dice*)

**Pattie** There's more to a meal than just cooking it, you know.

**Neville** (*counting out Clive's throw*) One, two, three, four.

**Clive** Damn.

**Phyllis** All right, next year I shan't cook anything. We'll leave it all to you, shall we?

**Pattie** Suits me. (*She goes out into the hall*)

**Phyllis** See how you get on, little Miss Know-all. (*She smiles to her companions*) See how she gets on, shall we?

**Neville** (*who has meanwhile been having his turn*) Three, four on a ladder. I'm on a ladder.

**Phyllis** Oh, you cheated.
**Neville** (*winking at Clive*) Nonsense.
**Phyllis** When I wasn't looking.
**Clive** No, he wasn't.
**Pattie** (*to herself*) Silly old bag. (*She looks round the hall*)
**Neville** I got four. See, one, two, three, four.
**Clive** Your turn. (*He pushes the dice to Phyllis*)
**Phyllis** Now, my turn.
**Pattie** Eddie? (*Calling back to the dining-room*) Has Eddie gone to bed?
**Neville** I think he's in the other room.
**Clive** Two, three and down a snake.
**Phyllis** (*with a cry*) Oh no.
**Neville** He's probably sleeping it off.
**Phyllis** Everyone's cheating. I'm the only one not cheating.
**Clive** My turn.

*They continue their game more quietly under the following. Pattie goes into the sitting-room. She goes to Eddie*

**Pattie** (*shaking him gently*) Eddie. Eddie, wake up. (*She sees Rachel for the first time*) Oh, I thought you'd gone to bed.
**Rachel** No.
**Pattie** We all thought you'd gone to bed.
**Phyllis** He's got another five. He's cheating.
**Pattie** (*shaking Eddie again*) Eddie. Why doesn't he ever learn? Eddie. He gets like this about once a month. Goes on the beer. I never know when he'll get back or who with.
**Neville** (*finishing his turn*) That's safe.
**Phyllis** My turn.
**Rachel** You mean, he brings other women home?
**Pattie** Oh no, nothing like that. No, he wouldn't do that. No, his mates, you know. He's got a lot of mates. They've all got wives who aren't as soft as I am. Can Bill sleep on our sofa, please? Because he's frightened to go home to his missus. You know . . .
**Phyllis** Why did I get a three? I didn't want a three.
**Pattie** Eddie. Eddie . . . You just have to keep shaking him like this. He wakes up after a bit.
**Rachel** I'd pick him up by his hair if I were you.
**Pattie** Oh no, you can't be too rough with him. He's only sick over you. Eddie. Eddie.

*A roar from the Snakes and Ladders players. Pattie and Rachel look up at the sound*

**Clive** (*excitedly*) Six, six, I got it!
**Neville** You lucky——
**Phyllis** I don't believe it.
**Neville** —so-and-so.
**Pattie** He's very nice, isn't he, your Clive? I mean, he's a bit quiet when you first meet him but he warms up.

**Rachel** Yes.

**Pattie** I expect he's quiet because he's busy remembering things for his book. But he's very nice. Nice eyes. He's all right, your Clive.

**Rachel** You really mustn't refer to him as my Clive. He's not my Clive.

**Pattie** Well, you know what I mean. Eddie. . . .

**Rachel** I'm not sure he'd care to be known as my Clive either. Poor man accepts an invitation from some Writers' Circle and suddenly finds himself saddled with the Secretary. Just too polite to say go away to her, that's all. Three awful dinners in three awful restaurants because I am not even capable of putting together a decent meal for us and that's our lot. So you can see, can't you, it really isn't anything serious. I'm sure he's wondering how on earth he came to be here.

**Pattie** He came, anyway, didn't he?

**Rachel** Oh yes. And now he's here, I'm sure he's delighted he came. But I don't flatter myself that's anything to do with me.

**Pattie** Eddie. Eddie.

**Rachel** So . . .

*During the above Phyllis has another turn. She now throws again*

**Phyllis** (*disappointed*) Oh, it's not fair. It's really not fair.

**Pattie** I don't know a lot about these things, mind you, but it seems to me that if you want something very badly you have to fight a bit.

**Rachel** Oh God.

**Pattie** You do. I had to fight for this. I did. You wouldn't believe it now but there were about four of us after him. I mean, we didn't really fight. It was all very polite really but I knew damn well I was going to get him and I did. Poor old Eddie, he didn't know anything about it. Still, he's got his own back now. Come on, Eddie, upsadaisy. Eddie, you're going to have to walk, love.

**Eddie** Yeh—yeh . . .

**Neville** Oh, that was ridiculous, I was nearly there.

*Phyllis screams with delighted laughter*

**Pattie** I can't carry you, you see, not when I'm like this.

**Eddie** I can walk—I can walk . . . (*As they go across the hall*) Did I tell you the news?

**Pattie** (*guiding him*) No, you haven't told me any news, Eddie. Mind where you're going.

**Phyllis** (*with a delighted cry*) Ha! Ha!

**Clive** Oh, look at that.

**Neville** The luck of the woman.

**Eddie** You want to hear my news?

**Pattie** Yes, I'd like to hear it very much. We've got the stairs now. Careful how you go.

**Eddie** I'm going to be a manager. A shop manager.

**Neville** (*as a triumphant cry*) Yes!

**Clive** No.

**Phyllis** No.

**Pattie** Oh yes, manager of what? (*She is more interested in getting him upstairs safely than in the conversation*)
**Eddie** Of a shop. I said of a shop.
**Phyllis** Nearly. I'm nearly there.
**Pattie** Yes, but what shop, Eddie?
**Eddie** Neville's. Neville's shop.
**Clive** No.
**Neville** No. Hard luck.
**Pattie** No, Nev's the manager, Eddie. He doesn't want another one.
**Eddie** He's opening a new shop. He's opening a new one.
**Neville** Oh hell's bells, look at that. Look at that.
**Pattie** Oh yes?
**Eddie** He told me. He's opening a new shop. Don't you believe me? Don't you believe me?
**Phyllis** (*preparing for her final throw*) Now then . . .
**Pattie** Yes, I think I do believe you, Eddie. I think I do. Now, quietly along here because of the kids.
**Eddie** Quietly now.
**Pattie** Quietly now.
**Eddie** Don't wake the kids.

*Eddie and Pattie go off upstairs*

*During the above, Rachel moves from her window-seat and slumps down in the armchair. As Eddie and Pattie go there is a final triumphant shout from the Snakes and Ladders players*

**Phyllis** (*very excitedly*) I've won. I've won. I'm the Champion Snakerer and Ladderer of all time.
**Neville** (*rising*) Cheat, cheat, cheat.
**Phyllis** Nonsense. (*To Clive*) You tell him I wasn't cheating.
**Clive** Absolutely disgraceful behaviour.
**Phyllis** (*absolutely delighted, mimicking him*) Absolutely disgraceful behaviour. I love this man. I adore him. Absolutely disgraceful behaviour. Say it again.
**Clive** Absolutely disgraceful behaviour.

*Phyllis screams with laughter. Neville stands in the doorway looking into the hall*

**Neville** (*calling*) Anybody about? (*Turning back to the others*) They've all gone to bed. Where's Harvey?
**Clive** I think he went upstairs when the film finished.
**Neville** That follows.
**Phyllis** Has my husband gone to bed?
**Neville** Looks like it.
**Phyllis** Good.
**Neville** (*moving to the middle of the hall*) Now then. God, I'm drunk. I've forgotten where the kitchen is. (*Remembering*) Oh yes.
**Phyllis** Absolutely disgraceful behaviour. I adore witty men. I love them.

*Bernard comes from the kitchen with a pair of very small wellington boots, on his way to the front door*

**Neville** Hallo, Bernard. You're looking well, mate.

**Bernard** (*a little taken aback by the bonhomie*) Yes?

*Bernard goes to the front door and leaves the wellingtons there. Neville starts for the stairs, and hesitates*

**Phyllis** (*to Clive*) My husband's not a witty man, you know. He's not witty at all.

**Clive** Oh dear.

**Neville** (*as Bernard returns*) My wife along there, is she?

**Bernard** Yes, she's just finishing off.

*Bernard goes off to the kitchen*

**Neville** (*following Bernard off*) Good old Belinda. Good old Bel. She's always somewhere finishing off.

*Neville goes off to the kitchen*

**Phyllis** (*to Clive*) Do you say a lot of witty things?

**Clive** Oh yes. Most of the things I say are extremely witty.

**Phyllis** God, that's wonderful.

**Clive** Wherever I go, people are generally rolling around all over the floor.

*Bernard returns from the kitchen, this time with two hot-water-bottles in rather ornate covers*

**Phyllis** Gracious.

**Bernard** (*arriving in the doorway*) Dearest . . .

**Phyllis** And that's what makes you a wonderful novelist, of course.

**Bernard** Dearest, I'm off now . . .

**Phyllis** Jolly good.

**Bernard** I've got the bottles. You won't be too long, will you?

**Phyllis** I just want to talk to this gentleman, dear, about his books.

**Clive** Well, perhaps it is getting a bit . . .

**Phyllis** No, no, no. I want to talk to you.

**Bernard** Don't be too long, will you, dear? Or you'll be up and down again.

**Phyllis** Good-night.

**Bernard** Yes, good-night, then.

**Clive** Night.

*Bernard goes across the hall and upstairs to bed*

**Phyllis** My husband's a doctor, you know. He's a brilliant doctor.

**Clive** Oh yes?

**Phyllis** But he's sacrificed his whole career to try and cure me. Isn't that an amazing story? When you write your next book, you really ought to write a book about my husband. There's a story there to be written, there really is. A man who gives up everything for the woman he loves. Isn't that a wonderful story?

**Clive** Oh yes.

*Neville enters from the kitchen with a glass of water*

**Phyllis** I'm going to tell you something really awful now.
**Clive** Oh?
**Phyllis** Now, you won't be shocked?

*Neville looks in on them*

**Neville** I'm off to bed now. Good-night.
**Phyllis** Good-night.
**Clive** Er . . . (*He makes as if to rise*)
**Phyllis** Sit down. You don't have to get up because he comes in.
**Neville** Glass of water. Drink a lot of water last thing at night you don't
    get a hangover. You don't get much sleep either but you don't get a
    hangover. Switch off there when you're through, will you?
**Phyllis** Yes, we will. Night-night.
**Neville** Night-night.

*Neville goes across the hall and up the stairs*

**Phyllis** Do you know. This is the awful thing. Do you know I haven't read
    your book. Isn't that awful?
**Neville** (*on the stairs*) God, I'm drunk.

*Neville goes off upstairs*

**Phyllis** Are you shocked?
**Clive** No.
**Phyllis** Really?
**Clive** Not at all. I think I'm probably the only person who has read my
    book actually. I had to. They kept sending me the proofs. I don't mind
    if you haven't read it. So long as you've bought it. Oh, Rachel's read it.
    I forgot Rachel.
**Phyllis** Oh yes. Poor Rachel. She reads everything. Nothing else to do.
    Now. I want you to teach me all about English Literature.
**Clive** What now?
**Phyllis** Please. Now. It's now or never. I realize I'm so ignorant. I'm
    thirty-nine years old. I know you wouldn't think that, but I'm thirty-
    nine years old and I want to know all about English Literature before
    it's too late.
**Clive** Well, I'm not really an expert.
**Phyllis** Let's start with you. What about you?
**Clive** Well . . .
**Phyllis** I'm dying to know. Where do your books come from? Are all
    those books up there then? (*She raps him on the forehead*) Waiting to
    come out.
**Clive** Book.
**Phyllis** What?
**Clive** Only one book. I've only written one book.
**Phyllis** No, I don't understand that. Tell me about you, then.
**Clive** Well, I was—um . . . Where do I start? My parents were . . .

**Phyllis** Are you a homosexual, for instance?
**Clive** Er—no—no, I'm not.
**Phyllis** That's a relief. A lot of them are, aren't they? Writers. Homosexuals.
**Clive** Well. I don't know. There's a proportion that are. But then there's a proportion in most professions. Probably no more than there are, say, train drivers.
**Phyllis** What?
**Clive** Train drivers.
**Phyllis** What are?
**Clive** Homosexuals.
**Phyllis** Are they?
**Clive** No.
**Phyllis** My God, I never knew that.
**Clive** No, that's not what I'm saying.

*Belinda enters from the kitchen*

**Phyllis** I mean, my God, those are great big machines, those trains . . .

*Belinda looks into the dining-room*

**Belinda** Good-night, I'm off to bed.
**Clive** Um . . .
**Phyllis** This man's been telling me extraordinary things about train drivers.
**Belinda** Really. Heavens. Would you switch off when you come up, please? You can leave the table lamp on in the hall. Just these and the landing lights, OK?
**Phyllis** Yes, we know.
**Belinda** Good-night, then.
**Clive** Good-night.
**Phyllis** Good-night. Go on, you were saying . . .

*Belinda switches off the Christmas tree lights at the base, also the hall overhead. She then goes upstairs and off*

**Clive** Look, everyone does seem to have gone to bed except us . . .
**Phyllis** You see, what I'm dying to ask you is, if you were a homosexual, do you think it would make a difference to the way you wrote?
**Clive** You mean, would I hold the pen slightly differently? (*He laughs*)
**Phyllis** No, I don't understand that. You're a very difficult man to get through to, do you know that? Are you a shy person?
**Clive** Well, I have—I have heard myself described as . . .
**Phyllis** (*rising*) Look, look, I want to show you something now they're all in bed. Quick, come with me.

*Phyllis moves uncertainly across the dining-room and out into the hall. Clive follows her, relieved at any rate to be clear of this room. He switches off the dining-room lights. Meanwhile Phyllis starts crawling about on her hands and knees at the base of the Christmas tree in amongst the presents*

**Clive** What are you doing?
**Phyllis** Just a minute. Just a minute. Want to find something. (*She shakes the odd parcel*) Find it in a minute.

**Clive** I don't think you should be doing that. I mean, they may be in a special order.

**Phyllis** Here we are. (*Producing a parcel*) This is it. This is it. (*Peering at the label*) "To darling Zoë with lots of love from Uncle Bernard and Auntie Phil." Look at this. I must show you this.

*She rips open the package and produces from its box one of those battery operated clockwork musical cuddly toys, possibly a drumming bear. Phyllis places it in the middle of the hall floor and switches it on. In the silence of the night, the noise seems quite deafening*

Look at him. Look at him. Isn't he marvellous? I couldn't resist him.

**Clive** Yes. Ssh. I'd switch him off now. I'd switch him off.

**Phyllis** I think it's a hoot. I think it's absolutely the funniest thing I've ever seen. You must put one in a book. (*She copies the toy doing a rival musical performance around the hall*)

*Harvey, in pyjamas and dressing-gown, appears at the top of the stairs*

**Harvey** I say. I say.

*Phyllis hides behind the Christmas tree. Clive dives for the toy and manages to switch it off*

I'm sorry to break things up down there but it is nearly one o'clock, you know.

**Clive** I'm sorry. We were just having a look at some presents.

**Phyllis** Having a look at some presents.

**Harvey** May I remind you there are also youngsters up here.

**Phyllis** Youngsters up here . . .

**Clive** Yes.

**Harvey** I'd be obliged.

**Phyllis** Obliged . . .

**Harvey** Who is that there? Is that Phyllis?

**Phyllis** Yes.

**Harvey** Is she all right?

**Clive** I think so.

**Harvey** I should get to bed. Things tend to start early on Boxing Day. Good-night.

**Clive** Good-night.

*Harvey goes off upstairs*

**Phyllis** Lord! What do you think he thought we were doing?

**Clive** I dread to think. We ought to go to bed, you know.

**Phyllis** (*indicating the wrapping paper*) Look at this. Look at all this.

**Clive** I'll do that. I'll pack it up again. You go to bed.

**Phyllis** You're sure?

**Clive** Yes. Please. Off you go.

**Phyllis** (*starting up the stairs*) Night-night, then.

**Clive** Good-night.

**Phyllis** *Bon soir.*

**Clive** Yes.

**Phyllis** *Buenos noches.*
**Clive** Sssh.
**Phyllis** *Gute Nacht.*
**Clive** Ssh.
**Phyllis** I'm glad you're not a train driver.
**Clive** No.

*Phyllis goes off upstairs*

*Clive, relieved, repacks the mechanical doll and wraps it as best he can. He is putting it carefully back where it came from, under the other presents, as Rachel comes out of the sitting-room*

**Rachel** (*who has the air of someone who has come to a sensible decision*) Look . . .
**Clive** (*startled*) Ah.
**Rachel** It's all right. Don't jump away. I'm not coming near you.
**Clive** No, I just—thought you'd gone to bed.

*Belinda appears at the top of the stairs, now in her dressing-gown and nightdress. She takes in the scene at a glance but does not falter. She comes briskly down the stairs*

**Belinda** Excuse me. I was just about to go to sleep and I think I've left the oven on.

*Belinda goes out to the kitchen*

**Rachel** (*after a pause*) No, I've been sitting in there and thinking things through.

*Belinda returns from the kitchen, marches straight past them and up the stairs without looking at them*

**Belinda** No. Thought I had. I hadn't. Thought I had. Night.
**Clive** Night.

*Belinda goes off upstairs*

**Rachel** (*after Belinda has gone*) I just wanted to say this. It's all right, it's quite simple. It won't take a second. It's this. What I want—need from you—and indeed I get from you is very different from what, say, Belinda wants from you. Or I think can give you. No, I'm not running her down or trying to be snide or anything. She's my sister, after all and I do recognize that probably her needs are much more normal than mine. Where I've been so stupid, though, is selfishly to expect us, you and me, to have one thing without the other. What I'm saying bluntly is that sex has played very little part in our brief relationship so far but it's well nigh impossible, I do see, for a man and a woman to carry on indefinitely without the subject at least cropping up. So, even if we succeeded platonically there would always be the Belindas of this world who'd sooner or later snap their fingers, destroy any relationship we'd built up in ten minutes . . .
**Clive** What you're saying is you want one but not the other.

**Rachel** Well, I've managed without the other extremely well for thirty-eight years. More or less. And I haven't honestly missed it and—well, I feel about it a bit like smoking—it would be stupid to take it up at my age and possibly damage my health when I've done so well so far. I hesitate to say all this to you because men usually take this terribly personally and feel hurt and hit back and accuse me of being frigid or a lesbian. Neither of which is true as it happens. I do feel some things very passionately quite often. And I don't fancy a woman cluttering up my bed any more than a man. Still, that's it. I realize I can't have only half so I'm handing you all back. I'm a bit drunk or I'd never have said this. I hope it makes sense. If I have hurt you, I'm very sorry because I wouldn't want to do that. Not for the world.

**Clive** I'm sorry too. We could—this all sounds very corny but I hope we can carry on in some sense. I really do value your friendship, you know.

**Rachel** Oh? Thank you.

**Clive** (*awkwardly*) All I'm saying is I wouldn't want to lose that. That's all.

**Rachel** No. Good. That's good. Good.

*Rachel suddenly caves in and starts to cry. Clive, for a moment, is transfixed with surprise*

**Clive** (*recovering*) Rachel . . . Now, Rachel, come on, now.

**Rachel** (*between sobs*) I'm sorry—I really am sorry. I never usually behave like this.

**Clive** (*beside her*) That's all right.

**Rachel** I really don't. You must believe me.

**Clive** No, no. I realize.

**Rachel** Oh, why does sex go and spoil everything? (*She sniffs*) God, I'm revolting. Have you got a . . .?

**Clive** No, I'm afraid . . .

**Rachel** No, you never do have one, do you? That little brown parcel there. (*She points to the base of the tree*) There's some in there, I think. Could you pass me one of those?

**Clive** (*getting them*) Right. (*Holding up the parcel*) This one?

**Rachel** Yes, I think so.

**Clive** (*tearing it open*) Yes, right first time. (*He pulls a handkerchief from the gift pack and hands it to Rachel*)

*Rachel blows her nose*

Better?

**Rachel** Thank you.

**Clive** I'll wrap these up again. Nobody'll know the difference. Whose are they?

**Rachel** (*starting to cry again*) They were my present to you.

**Clive** Oh, I see.

**Rachel** I had them embroidered specially because I knew you never had any. (*Wailing*) Now, you haven't got anything from me at all now.

**Clive** It's all right, Rachel. Look, I'm wrapping them up again. See?

**Rachel** (*getting louder*) Oh God, I'm such a mess, aren't I?

**Clive** (*as to a child*) Look, you see. (*By now he has wrapped them up again*) Now I've forgotten. You see? Forgotten what it is. Good heavens, what's this? No idea. Rachel, Rachel, please. (*He breaks off*)

*Harvey is back at the top of the stairs*

*Rachel turns, sees him, and quietens down*

**Harvey** What the hell is going on?
**Clive** Sorry.
**Harvey** One-thirty.
**Clive** Yes.
**Harvey** A.m.
**Clive** Yes. We were just wrapping presents.

*A sob from Rachel*

**Harvey** Who is that? Is that Rachel?
**Rachel** (*getting up, handkerchief clasped to her face*) Yes.

*She goes upstairs past Harvey*

**Clive** Rachel . . .
**Rachel** Good-night.
**Harvey** Good-night.
**Clive** Good-night.

*Rachel goes off upstairs*

**Harvey** I don't know what you're up to down there, Morris, but I'll say this, I can't say I've liked what I've seen. You take my tip, you'll buzz off to bed this minute.
**Clive** Yes. I'll just wrap this.
**Harvey** All right.

*Harvey goes off*

**Clive** Good-night.

*Clive finishes re-wrapping the handkerchiefs. He attempts to replace them where they were*

*As he is doing this, Belinda, briskly as before, comes downstairs barely taking Clive in*

**Belinda** (*to herself*) I know I left the deep-freeze open.

*Belinda goes off to the kitchen*

*Clive watches her off to the kitchen and is finishing his task when she returns*

*Belinda returns*

No. All's well. Up and down. Up and down, as Bernard would say. (*Pausing at the foot of the stairs*) Aren't you going to bed tonight?
**Clive** I'd hoped to. There were one or two distractions.
**Belinda** Yes, I heard some of them.
**Clive** Oh.

**Belinda** Sound tends to carry upwards in this hall, if you're not careful.
**Clive** (*lowering his voice*) Ah.
**Belinda** (*moving closer*) Well. I must be off. Up.
**Clive** Yes.

*They are very close*

**Belinda** (*in a whisper*) Oh God, I want you.
**Clive** I want you. (*He reaches out for her*)

*Belinda responds by clinging on to him fiercely. The following is all played
as softly as possible*

**Belinda** So much, so much . . .
**Clive** Ssh.
**Belinda** I need you.
**Clive** Yes, yes.
**Belinda** Come on, come on.
**Clive** Yes, yes. OK, OK.
**Belinda** I want you to make love to me now.
**Clive** Yes, OK.

*He half drags her across the hall to the sitting-room*

In here. Come on.
**Belinda** Now. Now.

*She kisses him repeatedly. He responds, in between trying to steer them both
through the sitting-room doorway*

I love you. I love you.
**Clive** I love you. This way, this way. That's it.
**Belinda** Please, please.
**Clive** Yes, all right. It's all right.

*He drops her into the chair*

I'll shut the door.
**Belinda** (*seeing where she is*) Oh God, no, not in here.
**Clive** Not in here?
**Belinda** Please not in here, it's our sitting-room.
**Clive** Why not?
**Belinda** I couldn't. Not in our sitting-room. Not in front of the television.
     Somewhere else.
**Clive** OK, OK. Come on.

*He pulls her up from the chair. She immediately responds by seizing hold of
him and starting to kiss him over again. During the following, Clive with
difficulty manages to reverse out of the sitting-room, across the hall to the
dining-room*

**Belinda** Let's go away together, please. Take me away. Take me with you,
     please.
**Clive** Yes, of course.
**Belinda** Just the two of us.

**Clive** Yes, yes.
**Belinda** Promise me you won't leave me.
**Clive** I won't leave you.

*They get to the dining-room. Clive gives it a quick glance and decides that that, too, is an unsuitable venue. He heads towards the kitchen*

**Belinda** I need you so much . . .
**Clive** Ssh. Ssh.
**Belinda** Want you, want you, want you . . .
**Clive** Hang on. Hang on.
**Belinda** Where are we going now?
**Clive** To the kitchen.
**Belinda** (*with a wail*) Oh, God, no, not in the kitchen.
**Clive** Ssh.
**Belinda** I'm not making love in a bloody kitchen. I'm too old for that.
**Clive** (*dragging her back into the hall*) Yes, all right. All right.
**Belinda** Here. Let's make love here.
**Clive** Here?
**Belinda** Please. Here. Please.
**Clive** (*laying her down*) Yes, all right, but quietly. We must be quiet.
**Belinda** Yes, I'll be quiet. We'll be quiet. Ssh.
**Clive** Ssh. That's it.

*They are lying now at the foot of the Christmas tree*

**Belinda** Oh my darling . . .
**Clive** (*fumbling with his belt*) Just a sec. Just a sec.
**Belinda** Dear God, you've got a beautiful body.
**Clive** Thank you.
**Belinda** Please be quick. (*She throws back her arms into a pile of Christmas presents*) Please.
**Clive** Yes.

*Belinda's gesture causes the musical toy to start up in its box. After the preceding whispered scene, it seems very loud indeed*

Ssh. Ssh.
**Belinda** What's that? What's that?
**Clive** It's that drumming bear.
**Belinda** Drumming what?
**Clive** Bear. Bear. It's a little bear that plays the drums. Find it quickly.
**Belinda** What the hell are you talking about?
**Clive** (*starting to rummage through the packages*) We'll have the whole house down here in a minute. It's one of these. (*He rips open the odd package*)
**Belinda** (*joining in and also ripping open parcels*) What does he look like?
**Clive** (*demonstrating*) He looks like this. Look, you'll recognize him I promise you. Where the hell is the little bastard?
**Belinda** I still don't know what we're looking for. (*Discovering a nasty pullover*) My God, who's this from? (*She checks the wrapper*)

**Clive**  Come on.

**Belinda**  This one's ticking.

**Clive**  Ticking?

**Belinda** (*reading*) "From Harvey to Bernard with resounding good wishes." Do you think he's planning to . . . (*She breaks off*)

*The Christmas tree lights flash on and off*

What was that?

**Clive**  Don't know.

*The lights come on again*

**Belinda**  Someone's doing it.

**Clive** (*producing Neville's control box from under him*) Hang on. I think it's this. Yes, look.

*The Christmas tree lights go off again*

**Clive**  You press this button and the lights come on. (*He demonstrates they do so*) See? And you press this one and they . . .

**Belinda** (*flinging the parcel she is holding from her and diving across at Clive*) Don't touch that one!

*She is too late. At the same moment as Uncle Harvey's alarm clock hits the floor and starts up very much as he promised, like a firebell, so Clive pushes the button and the children's Christmas song blares out from the tree. Clive drops the control unit*

(*Screaming*) Press it again! Press it again! (*She rummages in the paper looking for the unit*)

**Clive** (*above the din*) What the hell's happening?

**Belinda**  You've got to press the thing again! Turn it off.

**Clive**  What's that bell?

**Belinda**  Turn it off!

**Clive**  Who started that bell?

*Belinda finds the control box. Clive finds the bell. They silence them more or less simultaneously*

As they do so, the overhead hall light goes on. At the top of the stairs Harvey, Pattie, Rachel, Bernard, Neville and Phyllis, all in their night-wear, are now assembled looking down on them

**Belinda**  Oh.

**Clive**  Ah.

*Somewhere, in his box, the drumming teddy continues unabated. Clive stamps on a present rather at random. The drumming stops. A silence. Clive and Belinda stand breathless. The others stare back*

**Belinda** (*at length, rather feebly*) Sorry. We—just couldn't wait to open our surprises.

*They stand sheepishly. The others look distinctly unconvinced, as the Lights fade, and—*

                                        *the* CURTAIN *falls*

# ACT II

## SCENE 1

*The same. Mid-afternoon on Boxing Day*

*In the sitting-room, now set up in the corner by the window-seat, is Bernard's puppet theatre. Although the stage itself is simple, elaborate cardboard scenery is in the process of being set up. Bernard crawls around on his hands and knees doing this. His first scene is a village green. Pattie, his reluctant assistant, sits, bored, on the arm of the easy chair. She holds a pig puppet in one hand and a small dog puppet in the other. In the hall, the presents under the Christmas tree have gone. There is instead a red sack with the words "Father Christmas" on it containing a dozen small gift-wrapped presents. In the dining-room, the visible table has a practical cloth on it. It is in the process of being laid for a children's tea. At this end, however, Neville and Eddie have annexed a section and are busy repairing a piece of bear clockwork mechanism which twitches and jumps occasionally as they fiddle with it. Eddie's role is more of an assistant. He dutifully passes Neville any tool he asks for. Phyllis returns from the far end of the dining-table where she has placed one of two bowls of mousse. The other is already in view*

**Phyllis** (*to Neville*) You're not going to be on this table much longer, are you?

**Neville** (*very intent*) No, my love, no.

**Phyllis** Because we're trying to lay it for the children's tea, you know.

**Neville** Yes, yes. Just a tick. (*To Eddie*) Pass me that, would you? The small screwdriver.

*Phyllis clucks and goes back to the kitchen*

**Eddie** (*handing the screwdriver and staring into the works*) Do you think it's still fouling that?

**Neville** Could be. One way to find out. (*He performs a delicate mechanical task*)

*Rachel comes from the kitchen carrying a cardboard box containing paper hats, crackers and squeakers. She goes into the dining-room and starts to lay these out*

*Harvey, in the sitting-room, comes into view. He watches Bernard*

**Harvey** Thirty-seven minutes left.

**Bernard** All right.

**Rachel** (*working round Neville and Eddie*) Excuse me.

**Neville** (*without moving*) Sorry.

*Rachel continues her job*

**Harvey** I want this all to go smoothly. Run through your preview, then, when the kids arrive, they file in here and sit down in rows on the floor. How many are we expecting?

**Bernard** Just them and their friends. About a dozen, I think. The same as usual.

**Harvey** Two rows of six then. Right. They see the show—hooray, hooray —hopefully. As soon as that's finished, we'll open this door—(*indicating the sitting-room door*)—and there—(*he moves rapidly into the hall*)— here, standing by the tree who should there be but good old Father Christmas with his sack. Come and get your presents, kids.

*Rachel comes out of the dining-room*

And he'd better be here. I don't want to go routing him out of his shed like last year.

**Rachel** He's upstairs trying on his costume.

**Harvey** Who is?

**Rachel** Father Christmas. Clive Morris.

*Rachel goes out to the kitchen*

**Harvey** (*grimly*) Oh, it's him, is it? I don't like the sound of that. Then as soon as they're handed their presents, into here for tea. (*He moves to the dining-room door*) That'll work. (*To Neville*) More repairs?

**Neville** More repairs.

**Harvey** (*examining a bowl on the table*) Ah-ha. Jelly. Used to love jelly. Lucky kids.

**Eddie** How's the puppet show? Has he finished his preview?

**Harvey** Finished? It hasn't even started. Bloody silly old woman fiddling around with his curtains . . . (*He breaks off to stare at the bowl of mousse suspiciously*) Don't know what this is. It looks like mud.

**Eddie** It's very peaceful. Where are the kids?

**Harvey** They're out for a walk. I sent them down to the gravel pit.

**Neville** The gravel pit?

**Harvey** Yes. I told them to go and have a gun battle. Have a shoot-out with their new guns.

**Neville** Harvey, you're extremely bloodthirsty.

**Harvey** Why not? They've got to learn. There's going to come the time when any housewife who steps out of her front door without a loaded revolver in her basket will just be asking for trouble.

**Eddie** It'll make shopping in Tesco's quite exciting. Gunfight at the OK Sauce Corral. Bird's Custard's Last Stand. The Magnificent Seven-up . . .

**Harvey** Don't be so stupid. Stupid thing to say.

*Phyllis enters with a plate of sandwiches*

You won't be laughing about it when it happens.

*Phyllis places the plate on the table*

**Phyllis** What's that you're mending, Neville?

**Neville** Well, you remember that jolly little drumming bear, the one that accidentally got trodden on . . .

**Phyllis** That's not it.

**Eddie** He's undergoing surgery.

**Phyllis** Oh, I can't look. I think that's terrible. He's lost all his little personality.

**Neville** He's lost half his bloody little cogs as well.

**Phyllis** (*leaving the room*) I can't bear to look at that. I think that's terrible.

*Phyllis goes off to the kitchen*

**Harvey** (*shouting from the dining-room to the living-room*) Are you ready?

**Bernard** (*calling back*) No.

**Pattie** (*echoing this*) No.

**Harvey** (*drawing closer to Neville and Eddie, confidentially*) Listen, a word.

**Neville** Uh-huh?

**Harvey** This Morris man . . .

**Eddie** Who?

**Harvey** Clive Morris. This writer. What do you make of him?

**Neville** Make of him?

**Harvey** Well. Be honest. Last night, what about all that?

**Neville** I think we were all just a little bit merry last night, weren't we? I don't think we want to dwell too much on that. Nothing happened.

**Harvey** Nothing?

**Neville** I trust my wife.

**Harvey** Oh, I see. You mean, him and her?

**Neville** What else?

**Harvey** I wasn't meaning that. I meant the looting.

**Eddie** Looting?

**Harvey** Three times I caught him at it. Ripping open presents, helping himself to the contents.

**Eddie** Was he?

**Neville** Oh, come on.

**Harvey** I'm sorry. The man is a thief.

**Neville** No, Harvey, he is not a thief.

**Harvey** Look, I've had over thirty-five years in the security business. I know what I'm talking about. I've seen a million faces like his, sweating at you through a stocking mask. They're a type. You get to know them. The man's a con. Preying on single women like Rachel. One book, that's all he's written. Did you know that? Whoever heard of a writer who's only written one book, eh? Answer me that.

**Neville** He's all right, Harvey.

**Harvey** I'm watching him like a hawk. Night and day. Once they're in your house that's it. (*He paces a second*) And another thing, I hear he's going to be Father Christmas. Whose idea was that?

**Eddie** Nobody else wanted to do it.

**Neville** What's the harm?

**Harvey** Well, between us three, Phyllis had a chat with the man last night and she gathered and I trust her instincts, there's a strong possibility the man's a homosexual.

**Neville** Phyllis told you that?

**Harvey** He hangs about with engine drivers apparently.

**Eddie** I don't think I'm following this.

**Neville** I think it's very unlikely. Pass the pliers.

**Eddie** What's this bit about engine drivers?

*Belinda comes in from the kitchen and enters the dining-room. She brings in some sandwiches, covered*

*Harvey goes into the hall. His eye lights on the present sack. On a sudden impulse, he takes it up, seats himself in the hall, empties the contents on to the floor and starts to count them back into the sack*

**Belinda** Neville, for the tenth time, will you please move off the table.

**Neville** OK, OK.

**Belinda** You've got a workshop, why don't you—oh no, who put this out?

**Eddie** What?

**Belinda** What's the mousse doing out of the fridge? (*Yelling*) Phyllis? I wish to God that woman would stop helping me. Rachel and I could have done all this in ten minutes.

*Phyllis comes from the kitchen*

**Phyllis** Hallo, do I hear my name?

**Belinda** Phyllis, this is frozen mousse, dear, frozen. For their pudding. They are not due to eat until after Bernard's show finishes and that could be any time between now and New Year's Eve.

**Phyllis** I didn't know it was mousse.

**Belinda** Then what do you think it was doing in the fridge?

**Phyllis** (*going off, injured, with the two bowls*) I didn't know it was mousse, did I?

*Phyllis goes to the kitchen*

*Belinda goes to the other end of the table with her plate of sandwiches*

**Neville** (*oblivious of all this*) Yes, that's moving more freely.

**Eddie** Good.

*Pattie rises from the chair in the sitting-room*

**Neville** I think we might start reassembling it, now, don't you?

**Pattie** (*picking up the scissors*) You finished with these?

**Bernard** Mm. Mm.

**Pattie** I'll take them back then. (*She moves to the sitting-room doorway*)

**Bernard** Don't go too far, I'm nearly ready.

**Pattie** Oh, hooray.

*Belinda returns to view*

**Belinda** Out in one minute, please, Nev.

**Neville** Right.

*Belinda leaves the dining-room and meets Pattie in the hall. Harvey finishes his count of Christmas presents*

**Harvey** (*dumping down the sack on the floor*) Twelve. There's twelve presents in there.

**Belinda** I hope so. There's twelve children. There should be. (*To Pattie*) I'll take those. (*She takes the scissors from her*)

**Pattie** Thanks. I'm fed up with sitting in there.

*Belinda picks up the present sack and returns it to the base of the tree. Once there, she starts to trim the tree with the scissors*

**Harvey** (*to Pattie*) Tell him he's got thirty-two minutes left.

**Pattie** He's nearly ready,

**Harvey** I don't believe it. (*To Belinda*) Did you hear that? He's ready.

**Belinda** (*still absorbed with the tree*) Yes, I've just got to finish out there, Harvey.

**Harvey** (*sticking his head into the dining-room*) He's ready now. You can come in. Show's about to start.

**Neville** It's a bit tricky at the moment, Harvey. We'll be along in a second.

**Eddie** In a second.

**Harvey** Well, it's about to start. (*Shouting to the house in general*) Preview's about to start. (*To Belinda*) Where's Phyllis?

**Belinda** In the kitchen destroying something, I should think.

**Harvey** Right, I'll fetch her.

*Harvey goes off to the kitchen*

**Belinda** Please do. Get her out of my kitchen.

*During the above Pattie stands in the hall watching Belinda absently*

How are you? You're looking better today.

**Pattie** Yes, I feel better. More positive.

**Belinda** Good.

**Pattie** I think Eddie's news helped.

**Belinda** News?

**Pattie** Nev's offered him a job. Did you know that?

**Belinda** Oh, he has. Good, I knew he was going to. Is Eddie going to take it.

**Pattie** Oh, I think he will. I'm sure he will.

**Belinda** Good.

**Pattie** He couldn't afford to let a job like that go, could he? Not a managership.

**Belinda** Managership?

**Pattie** That's what he's offered him. Manager of the—you know—(*secretively*)—the new shop.

**Belinda** Oh.

*Harvey enters from the kitchen*

**Harvey** She's crying about something. I don't know what. Mousse, I think she said.

**Pattie** You sound surprised.

**Belinda** (*recovering*) No, I just didn't realize he was making him the manager. Super.

*Harvery goes into the sitting-room*

**Pattie** Oh yes, definitely. Eddie said.

**Bernard** Come on, then.

**Harvey** Come on.

**Pattie** I'm coming.

**Belinda** Yes.

*Belinda goes back to the kitchen, rather thoughtful*

*Pattie returns to the sitting-room.*

**Harvey** Right.

**Bernard** Are they coming?

**Harvey** No.

**Bernard** They're not coming?

**Harvey** Just us.

**Bernard** What about Phyllis?

**Harvey** Yes, she'll probably be in, she said. Soon as she's cleaned some mousse off the floor. For the time being, I'm afraid I'm your only audience. So get on with it. Entertain me.

*Harvey spins round the armchair so that it now faces the puppet stage and prepares to sit*

**Bernard** (*alarmed*) Don't sit on those.

**Harvey** Whoops. Jolly good start, eh? Audience enters and sits on the cast.

**Pattie** (*retrieving her two puppets from the chair*) I'll take those.

**Bernard** Now, I've got the characters over here. (*He indicates the rail at one side like a small low clothes rail on which hang a dozen or so puppets*) And the scenery I'm keeping on this side. (*He indicates a stack of cardboard scenery*) Now, all I want you to do is to be ready to pass me either a character or a piece of scenery as I ask for it.

**Pattie** There's an awful lot of this. Don't we need someone else?

**Bernard** No, no. Too many people and you're all in each other's way. It's hopeless. The less the better. Now. Off we go. Your first job will be to do the curtain. (*He indicates a string*) You pull this for the curtain, all right?

**Pattie** Right. (*She pulls it*)

**Harvey** (*as the curtain goes up*) Hooray.

**Bernard** Not yet, not yet. Let it down, let it down. I'm not ready.

**Pattie** Oh. (*She does so*)

**Harvey** (*as the curtain goes down again*) Boo.

**Bernard** Oh, do be quiet, Harvey.

**Harvey** You've got twenty-eight minutes until the audience arrives.

**Bernard** All right. I haven't got my beginners. Pass me the postman and the pig.

**Pattie** (*hunting through the rail of puppets*) Postman and a pig.
**Bernard** And then I'll need second pig very shortly. I'll keep hold of postman but you be ready to take first pig from me when he comes off and then hand me second pig.
**Pattie** (*handing him puppets*) Postman and pig.
**Bernard** No, no, that's second pig. I want first pig. That pig. That one there.
**Pattie** (*to Harvey*) Wrong pig.

*Bernard holds the postman while Pattie replaces the second pig and looks for the first pig*

These pigs all look the same. (*She finds it*)
**Harvey** Twenty-seven minutes.
**Bernard** Oh shut up. Do shut up.

*Eddie, still watching Neville, uncovers the sandwiches and starts to eat them*

All right and curtain—UP.

*Pattie pulls up the curtain and wonders what to do with the string in her hand. Bernard walks the postman on to the village green set*

(*In the postman's voice*) Well, well, well. Hallo, children.
(*Aside to Pattie*) Tie it on the hook. On the hook there.
**Pattie** Oh. (*She does so*)
**Bernard** (*in the postman's voice*) Hallo there, children.
**Harvey** Hallo.
**Bernard** (*in the postman's voice*) Oh dear, that's not a very big hallo. Bet you can make a bigger hallo than that. Let's hear a big hallo. Hallo, children.
**Harvey** (*roaring in a terrible voice*) Hallo! Get on with it!
**Bernard** (*a little taken aback. In the postman's voice*) Yes, that's better. Well, isn't this a lovely day to be a postman here on the village green. (*Singing*) Pom pom de dom.

*He brings on the first pig*

(*In the postman's voice*) Well, good day, Mr Pig. And what's your name, may I ask?
(*In the first pig's voice*) If you please, Mr Postman, my name is Hubert Pig. And I'm off to build my house. And I'm looking for some straw to build it with. Good day.
(*In the postman's voice*) Oh, I see. Well, well. Good day.
(*In the first pig's voice*) Good day.

*Bernard walks the first pig off*

(*To Pattie, aside*) Second pig, quickly, second pig.
(*In the postman's voice*) Pom pom de dom.

*During this there is a hurried exchange between Pattie and Bernard. She hands him the second pig and takes the first pig from him. Bernard brings on the second pig. Pattie hangs up the first pig*

(*In the postman's voice*) Good morning, Mr Pig, what's your name, may I ask?

(*In the second pig's voice*) If you please, Mr Postman, my name is Wilfred Pig. And I'm off to build my house. And I'm looking for some sticks to build it with. Good day.

(*In the postman's voice*) Oh, I see. Well, well. Good day.

(*He walks the second pig off. Aside to Pattie*) Third pig, quickly, third pig.

**Pattie** (*taken by surprise*) *Third* pig? (*She grabs a pig from the rail*)

**Bernard** (*in the postman's voice*) Well, good day, Mr Pig and what's your . . .

(*He whips the pig off the stage again. To Pattie aside*) This is the first pig again. I said the third pig.

**Harvey** What happened there? A pig shot on and off.

**Bernard** Wait. Wait. (*To Pattie, indicating the pig he wants*) That one.

**Harvey** Twenty-five minutes to go.

**Bernard** That's third pig.

**Pattie** Unless you know them very well, Bernard, it's hard to tell the difference. Honestly.

*Bernard takes the third pig from her and gives her the first pig. Pattie hangs the first pig up. Bernard walks on the third pig*

**Bernard** (*in the postman's voice*) Pom pom de dom. Well, good morning, Mr Pig.

**Harvey** (*under his breath*) Oh, dear God.

**Bernard** (*in the postman's voice*) What's your name, may I ask?

(*In the third pig's voice*) If you please, Mr Postman, my name is Ginger Pig and I'm off to build my house and I'm looking for some bricks to build it . . .

**Harvey** Ginger?

**Bernard** What?

**Harvey** Is that his name? Ginger?

**Bernard** What's wrong with it? Hubert, Wilfred and Ginger.

**Harvey** Bit weak for a pig, isn't it? Ginger?

**Bernard** That's what he's called.

**Pattie** Look, can we get on, please?

**Harvey** It's not at all convincing. Ginger pig.

**Bernard** (*finishing off rather sulkily. In the third pig's voice*) Going to build my house and I'm looking for some bricks to build it with, good day.

(*Aside to Pattie, handing her the third pig*) Right, take him.

(*In the postman's voice*) Well, well, well. What do you know? Three little pigs. All going to build their houses. Pom pom de dom.

(*To Pattie, who is hanging up the third pig still*) Curtain down. Curtain.

(*In the postman's voice*) Pom pom de dom.

(*To Pattie*) Come on, come on.

**Pattie** All right. I can't do two things at once.

**Bernard** (*in the postman's voice*) Pom pom de dom.

*Pattie drops the curtain*

**Harvey** (*applauding brusquely*) Jolly good. Well, it's certainly shorter than Ali-Baba, isn't it? Which is all to its credit. I still think you can trim it a bit. What about cutting out that ginger pig?

**Bernard** That's not the end.

**Harvey** Isn't it?

**Bernard** That's only Scene One.

**Harvey** You mean there's more?

**Bernard** Of course.

**Harvey** How much more?

**Bernard** There's sixteen scenes.

**Harvey** Sixteen?

**Bernard** Yes. (*To Pattie*) Come on, come on. Change the scenery.

**Harvey** Well, you've got twenty-two minutes and then it's your gala opening. So get your skates on.

**Bernard** Now then.

*Bernard and Pattie busy themselves changing the scenery. It is an involved operation and requires removing all the existing scenery, in this case the village green and replacing it with another equally involved setting: in this case the wolf's lair. Harvey rises*

**Harvey** Well, if it's an interval, I'll take a stroll.

*Harvey leaves the sitting-room*

*Clive, in full Father Christmas kit plus beard, comes downstairs. Harvey stops and looks at him suspiciously*

**Clive** Hallo.

**Harvey** Good afternoon. Got up at last, have you?

**Clive** That's right.

*Harvey continues to stare at him. Clive adjusts his beard self-consciously*

Well . . . (*Seeing the sack of presents, in jovial Father Christmas tones*) Oh-ho-ho-ho, these must be mine. (*He goes to pick up the sack*)

**Harvey** (*in a low tone*) I thought you'd like to know I've counted every one of those presents in that sack.

**Clive** Oh, have you really?

**Harvey** Thought you'd like to know. (*He strolls back into the sitting-room, past Bernard*)

**Bernard** Nearly ready . . .

**Harvey** Time you've finished, your audience will have grown up and left home.

*They work on in silence. Harvey wanders further into the sitting-room and out of view. Clive, uncertain where to go next, wanders to the door of the dining-room. He stops short as he sees Neville and Eddie*

**Clive** Ah. Hallo.

**Eddie** Afternoon.

**Clive** Hallo.

**Neville** (*without looking up*) Good afternoon.

**Eddie** You're up then.

**Clive** Yes, I've—er . . .

**Eddie** Haven't shaved yet, though, have you, eh? (*He laughs*)

**Clive** What? Oh—(*he laughs*)—no.

**Neville** Pass me that, would you?

**Eddie** (*holding up a piece of mechanism*) This?

**Neville** That's the one. Ta.

*They work on. Clive wanders back into the hall feeling rather spare. In the sitting-room Harvey appears in view with the "Radio Times" in his hand. Bernard takes the wolf puppet and the dog puppet from the rack*

**Harvey** My God, I didn't know that was on tonight. Wonderful stuff.

**Bernard** Right. Ready with the curtain.

**Pattie** Ready with the curtain.

*Harvey resumes his seat hurriedly*

**Bernard** And curtain—UP.

*Rachel comes from the kitchen with a plate of chocolate biscuits*

*Pattie pulls up the curtain and ties it off, as Bernard whispers something to her*

**Rachel** (*seeing Clive, pleasantly*) Oh, good morning. Afternoon.

**Clive** Hallo.

*Pattie flashes the sitting-room lights on and off several times to simulate lightning whilst Bernard makes thunder noises. The following occurs more or less simultaneously*

**Rachel** That looks OK. Thanks so much for doing it.

**Harvey** Took three minutes forty-six seconds, that scene change . . .

**Clive** I promised yesterday I'd do it. I'll do it. It seems to be the very least I can do after . . . (*He remembers*)

**Bernard** Woo-harr—I am the evil wolf and this is my lair—har-har . . .

**Clive** Oh, God—Rachel . . .

**Bernard** (*making a small dog barking noise*) Row-ruff-ruff-row . . .

**Rachel** Would you like a cup of tea?

**Bernard** (*in the wolf voice*) Who is that at the door of my lair, har?

**Clive** I've been sitting up there—thinking a lot about what you said last night and . . .

**Bernard** (*in the dog voice*) Ruff-ruf-row-row . . .

**Rachel** Coffee. Have some coffee.

**Clive** Oh, well. Coffee. Please. Listen Rachel . . .

**Rachel** Won't be a minute.

**Bernard** Why it's my little dog Waggums. Come in, Waggums.

**Harvey** Waggums?

*Rachel goes into the dining-room and puts her biscuits on the table. Clive makes to follow her, realizes this is no use, and waits*

**Rachel** (*in the dining-room*) You still here?

**Neville** We're going. We're going.
**Bernard** (*in the wolf voice*) Come here—come to your master—har-har . . .
**Harvey** Now this is the one who should have been called Ginger.

*Rachel comes out of the dining-room*

**Clive** Rachel, about last night, I——
**Bernard** (*in the dog voice*) Ruff-ruff-row-row . . .
**Rachel** (*going towards the kitchen*) You don't take sugar, do you?
**Clive** No. I . . .
**Bernard** (*in the dog voice*) Row-row-row . . .
**Rachel** (*cheerfully*) Good.

*Rachel goes off to the kitchen*

*Clive wanders and then sits in the hall, confused and unhappy*

**Bernard** (*in the wolf voice*) Har, what are you telling me, Waggums? Three
little pigs have decided to build houses?
(*In the dog voice*) Row-row-ruff-ruff.
(*In the wolf voice*) In the village, eh? Well, let me have a brief nap first.
Then I'll be off. To blow down their houses and eat them.
**Harvey** Eat their houses?
**Bernard** No, the pigs.
(*In the wolf voice*) Now for my nap. Snore. Snore.

*Bernard does business with the dog*

(*Making a musical sound*) Dee. Deedee. Dee. Bomp. (*He walks the dog
up to the wolf and nudges him as he sleeps*)
(*In the wolf voice*) Har. Whassat? Whassat? Snore.

*Bernard repeats the business*

Dee. Deedee. Dee. Bomp.
(*In the wolf voice*) Har. Whassat? Whassat? Snore.
**Harvey** How long is this going on for?
**Bernard** Just a minute.
**Harvey** He's done that twice.
**Bernard** Why shouldn't he?
**Harvey** Because it's excruciatingly boring. What's all this deedee bomp?
**Bernard** It's comic relief.
**Pattie** It's quite a good bit this, Harvey. I like this bit.
**Bernard** There you are.
**Harvey** If I were the wolf, I'd eat that bloody dog for a kick-off.
**Pattie** Go on, Bernard.

*Bernard continues his wolf/dog business as before*

*Phyllis comes out from the kitchen during this*

**Phyllis** (*muttering*) All right. Do it all yourself then. Do it all yourself.
(*Seeing Clive, coolly*) Oh, good afternoon.
**Clive** Hallo.
**Phyllis** Sobered up yet, have we?

**Clive** We should have done, shouldn't we?

*Phyllis goes into the sitting-room. Bernard's interminable comic business is continuing*

**Phyllis** (*creeping across the room, finger to her lips and whispering*) Am I late?
**Harvey** No. Come and sit down. You're just in time to see the end of this dog.

*Harvey offers her his chair. Phyllis sits and begins, almost at once, to laugh delightedly*

**Bernard** (*in the wolf's voice*) Snore.
    (*In the dog's voice*) Ruff-ruff. Snore snore.
**Harvey** Snore.
**Bernard** And—curtain.

*Pattie lets in the curtain*

**Phyllis** Oh, that's not the end?
**Bernard** No, no.
**Harvey** You're in luck, there's another fourteen scenes yet.
**Phyllis** You better hurry up, dear. They'll be here in quarter of an hour.
**Bernard** (*starting to change the scenery*) Now, don't you start, Phyllis, I'm going as quick as I can.
**Phyllis** All right, dear. (*To Harvey*) Have I taken your chair?
**Harvey** I'll get another.

*Harvey goes off into the unseen part of the sitting-room. Pattie and Bernard labour on*

    *Belinda comes in from the kitchen with paper napkins*

*Clive rises as he sees her*

**Clive** Hallo.
**Belinda** (*briskly*) Hallo. (*She goes into the dining-room*)

*Clive sits. Belinda sees Neville and Eddie*

    Oh God, Nev, please.
**Neville** All right.
**Belinda** How many times do I have to ask you?
**Neville** (*rising*) I'm going now. You see. I'm going now. (*He gathers up some immediate bits but leaves the rest for Eddie*) Eddie, could you kindly bring the rest of the stuff?

    *Neville goes out to the kitchen, watched by Clive*

**Eddie** Certainly.
**Belinda** (*to Eddie*) Have you been eating these? (*She indicates the sandwiches*)
**Eddie** One or two.

*Belinda, exasperated, snatches up the plate and takes it to the far end of the table. Simultaneously, Harvey brings an upright chair from presumably the other side of the sitting-room and places it next to Phyllis and sits. Eddie gathers up all the bits into a box, and starts to leave the dining-room*

**Phyllis** That's better, Harvey. (*To Bernard*) Are you going to be long, dear?

**Bernard** (*frustratedly, as his scenery falls down again*) Oh, damn it. What's the matter with this?

**Harvey** Twelve minutes. (*He wanders off again into the far sitting-room*)

**Pattie** Why don't we get some help?

**Phyllis** You could do with some help.

**Pattie** (*rising*) We need another man. This is all too technical. (*She goes into the hall*)

**Bernard** (*feebly*) The more people we—oh . . .

*Pattie meets Eddie coming out of the dining-room*

**Pattie** Eddie. Eddie, could you come please?

**Eddie** I'm helping Nev.

**Pattie** Eddie, please.

**Eddie** I've got this.

**Pattie** If you don't come, we're going to be at this all night. Please, please, Eddie.

*During this, Neville returns along the passage*

**Eddie** Oh, blimey.

**Neville** What's the matter?

**Eddie** Can I give you these? I've got to help them.

**Pattie** (*deeply grateful*) Thank you, Eddie.

**Neville** (*taking the box from Eddie*) Fair enough.

**Pattie** I don't understand these things, you see.

**Eddie** (*following her into the sitting-room*) Well, I don't. Now, Bernard, what's the trouble?

**Bernard** Just a minute. I've done it, I think.

*His scenery falls down*

No I haven't.

*Pattie sits on the window-seat. Eddie crouches beside Bernard to see if he can help. Clive approaches Neville in the hall. Neville hunts through the box, looking for something*

**Clive** Look—Neville . . .

**Neville** Santa? What can I do for you?

**Clive** Something has to be said about last night.

**Neville** No need.

**Clive** I think there is.

**Neville** We were all drunk. You were drunk, she was drunk. So was I. Forget it.

**Clive** Look, we really weren't that drunk.

**Neville** I think I'd prefer it if you were.

**Clive** Sorry?

**Neville** (*quietly and pleasantly*) Let's put it this way. If I thought for one moment that you'd been down there on my floor in my hall under my Christmas tree, trying to screw my wife while you were both stone-cold sober, that would put a very different complexion on things. Because in that case, I promise you I would start to take you to pieces bit by bit. And as for her, she'd find herself back on Social Security before she had time to pull her knickers up. OK, Santa? (*He winks at Clive*) Good lad.

*Neville pats Clive on the shoulder and goes out along the kitchen passage-way*

*Clive stands bemused. Belinda comes back into view in the dining-room, having rearranged the table. She now leaves the room and moves past Clive to the kitchen*

**Clive** Er . . .

**Belinda** (*turning*) Yes?

**Clive** Nothing.

**Belinda** No. Right.

*Belinda goes back to the kitchen*

*Clive sits on the bench in the hall. Bernard stands up triumphantly in the sitting-room, the scenery staying in place*

**Bernard** There.

**Phyllis** You've done it. Well done.

**Pattie** Hooray.

**Bernard** On we go.

**Phyllis** We're going on.

**Harvey** (*reappearing*) You have a little over nine minutes to do fourteen scenes.

**Bernard** Don't be ridiculous.

**Harvey** True.

**Bernard** Right. I want Waggums, then the wolf, then first pig, all right?

**Pattie** Right. Here's Waggums. (*She hands him the dog*)

**Eddie** What am I doing?

**Bernard** You can help with the transformation.

**Eddie** The what?

**Bernard** And curtain—UP.

*Pattie pulls up the curtain*

**Phyllis** Hooray, look, it's a little haystack. Look.

**Bernard** No, it's not. It's his house. It's a straw house.

**Phyllis** Oh yes.

**Bernard** (*in the dog voice*) Row-row-ruff-ruff-ruff.

**Harvey** Oh no, the funny dog's back again.

**Bernard** (*in the dog voice*) Row-row—wolf—wolf—row-row.

(*To Pattie*) Wolf! Wolf! Pattie, wolf.

*Pattie barks in "the wings"*

Wolf, Pattie, wolf!

**Pattie** Wolf. I'm sorry. I thought you said woof. Here. (*She hands him the wolf*)

**Bernard** (*in the wolf's voice*) Har-har.

**Pattie** (*catching the scenery with her stomach*) Whoops.

**Phyllis** Oh dear.

*Eddie replaces it*

**Pattie** Sorry . . .

**Bernard** Careful. Would you kindly watch your stomach.

**Pattie** I can't help it, can I?

**Bernard** Well, hold it in. Can't you hold it in?

**Pattie** No, I can't hold it in. If I could hold it in I would.

**Bernard** All right.

**Phyllis** She's pregnant, Bernard.

**Bernard** (*savagely*) Shut up! I'm sorry, dear. I'm sorry.

**Harvey** That dog is now three feet off the ground.

**Bernard** All right.

**Harvey** He's now lost all credibility.

**Bernard** (*in the wolf voice*) Har-har. So this is the little straw house, Waggums.

**Eddie** (*whispering to Pattie*) Shall I keep holding this?

**Pattie** (*crossly*) I don't know. Don't ask me.

**Eddie** Right. (*He continues to support the back piece*)

**Bernard** (*ploughing on. In the wolf voice*) We'll soon blow this down. Har-har-har. Hallo, Mr Pig. Mr Pig . . .
(*Aside to Pattie*) Pig. First pig.

**Pattie** Oh God, first pig. (*She hurriedly tries to find it*)

**Bernard** Stupid girl. She's stupid. Stupid.

**Phyllis** I love that little thing in the corner.

**Harvey** Where?

**Phyllis** There. That little animal in the corner. It's like a little caterpillar. It's terribly well made.

**Eddie** (*who along with everyone else is peering round the front to see*) That's my thumb.

**Bernard** Come on, come on. Quick. Quick, quick.

**Pattie** (*finding a pig*) Here. Here.

*Pattie hurries round with a pig to give to Bernard*

**Bernard** (*in the first pig voice*) Hallo, who's there? Who's that knocking on my . . .

*Pattie knocks the scenery again with her stomach*

You silly, stupid woman. You stupid—silly—clumsy—silly—stupid —woman . . .

**Phyllis** Bernard—dear . . .

**Bernard** You see what she did—you see what she did . . .

**Harvey** Six minutes.

**Pattie** (*thrusting the pig at Bernard*) Do you want this or don't you?

*Bernard snatches the pig ungraciously from her*

**Bernard** (*in the first pig voice*) Hallo. Who's that knocking on my . . .

*He snatches the pig out of the scene*

    (*Aside to Pattie*) This is the wrong pig again. Why do you keep giving me the wrong pig, you fool?

**Pattie** (*tearfully*) Don't you keep calling me a fool . . .

**Harvey** There we are. We've had it all now. Flying pigs. (*He studies the "Radio Times"*)

**Bernard** How can I do the show properly if these stupid people keep handing me the wrong pigs?

**Pattie** How am I supposed to tell the bloody difference?

**Bernard** (*screaming and waving a pig at her*) Pig one. Pig one. This is pig one.

**Eddie** (*getting up and letting go of the scenery which promptly falls down*) Don't you shout at her like that.

**Pattie** You find your own stupid pigs. (*She stamps out in tears and starts to go upstairs*)

**Phyllis** Bernard, dearest, if you'd . . .

**Bernard** (*screaming at Phyllis*) Shut up.

*Bernard sits on the edge of his stage his head in his hands*

**Phyllis** (*very agitated*) Oh dear. Oh dear. I wish he wouldn't shout.

**Eddie** Well, that's that, isn't it? That's that.

*Eddie goes out into the hall. Pattie has gone three-quarters of the way up the stairs, and now sits down on a step. Eddie looks up and sees her*

    Pattie?

*Pattie continues to sit without reacting*

    Pattie?

**Pattie** Yes?

**Eddie** Look . . . (*He considers going to join her for a second*) If you—if you want me, I'll be out with Nev, OK?

**Pattie** (*looking at him briefly*) OK.

**Eddie** Right.

*Eddie goes out to the kitchen*

*Clive, who sitting in the hall, is party to all this, tries to remain unobtrusive. Bernard gets up*

**Phyllis** Are you going on, dear?

**Bernard** I don't know what to do.

**Harvey** (*looking up from the "Radio Times"*) Well, you've got three minutes so make up your mind.

**Bernard** (*suddenly angry*) Oh, don't be idiotic, Harvey. How can I finish this play off in three minutes? Don't be so idiotic.

**Harvey** (*rising impatiently*) Come on, then, I'll show you. I'll show you how to finish your play. It's perfectly simple. Give me those. (*He grabs the pig and the wolf from Bernard*)

**Bernard** Watch what you're doing.

**Phyllis** Careful, Harvey, mind him.
**Harvey** Here's your ending. Har-har-har, hallo, Mr Pig. I've come to eat
you. Really, Mr Wolf? Well, take that. Bash, bam, wallop, biff, whack.

*Harvey crashes the puppets together with great savagery, simulating a fight.
This culminates with him hurling the wolf high in the air so that it lands some
distance away in the corner of the room, a tangle of limbs and strings.
Harvy kicks the scenery in the theatre over for good measure, then stands
triumphant*

End of wolf. Good enough for you?

*A silence*

**Phyllis** (*crying*) He took so much care making those.
**Bernard** (*in a deep rage now, his voice low and controlled*) You are a loath-
some man, Harvey, you really are. You're almost totally negative, do
you know that? And that's such an easy thing to be, isn't it? So long as
you stay negative, you're absolutely safe from laughter or criticism
because you've never made anything or done anything that people can
criticize. All they can really say about you is that you're a snob, a bigot,
a racist, a chauvinist, an ignorant, insensitive, narrow-minded, intolerant,
humourless wart.
**Harvey** (*having digested this*) Very well. We shall see. We'll see who's
negative. Ha!

*Harvey goes out into the hall*

*Rachel comes along from the kitchen with a cup of coffee. She stops as
she sees Harvey*

We'll see. (*Speaking to the house in general*) You'll all be glad of me
sometime. Laugh now but you'll see.

*Harvey goes out by the front door*

*Bernard crouches down by his theatre, retrieves the pig Harvey has dropped
and sits on the floor untangling it*

**Rachel** (*coming further into the hall*) Oh dear, dramas?
**Clive** Apparently.
**Rachel** (*handing him the coffee*) Oh dear. There. I warned you it'd take
ages. It takes a woman like me to make a mockery of the words instant
coffee. (*She goes into the dining-room and takes some spoons from the
sideboard drawer*)
**Phyllis** What are you going to do, dear?
**Bernard** I don't know. I don't know.
**Clive** Rachel ...
**Rachel** Yes?
**Clive** Just a minute, please.

*Rachel comes back into the hall*

**Rachel** Listen, Clive, if you're going to say something of great importance
to me, do you think you could possibly take that beard off?

**Clive** (*removing it*) Oh, damn it.
**Rachel** It'll make it easier to drink your coffee, as well.
**Clive** I just want you to know whatever anyone says I wasn't drunk last night.
**Rachel** Weren't you? I was.
**Clive** Look. Last night . . .
**Rachel** Yes?
**Clive** You mustn't blame yourself, Rachel. You really mustn't.
**Rachel** No.
**Clive** I understand, you see. God, I'm a writer, I should understand, after all. If I don't understand . . . You'd been feeling guilty because you felt that you'd been holding back on me—failing to give me what you felt I needed from you. Am I right?
**Rachel** Yes, I think so. I don't . . .
**Clive** But, Rachel, you must understand—what you felt that I needed from you—that part of you that you felt I needed to have from you—yourself, if you like . . .
**Rachel** Yes?
**Clive** Well, you see, Rachel, I never wanted it.
**Rachel** Oh.
**Clive** Not from you.
**Rachel** Ah.
**Clive** So what I'm saying is you mustn't feel guilty.
**Rachel** No.
**Clive** And if I gave you the impression that I did. Want what I thought you thought I did. I'm sorry. It was my fault, that's all.
**Rachel** Yes.
**Clive** (*with sudden passion*) God, I need to go away and just sit and try and sort myself out. I'll do this for you. And the kids. Then I'll go. I'll creep away to the railway station and vanish from your life.
**Rachel** You'll be sitting there for a long time if you go now. There's no trains till tomorrow.
**Clive** Oh, hell. I'll catch the first one in the morning.
**Rachel** The first one?
**Clive** Yes.
**Rachel** That's at six-oh-six.
**Clive** Perfect.
**Rachel** Nobody catches the six-oh-six.
**Clive** I will.
**Rachel** (*returning to the dining-room*) OK, I'll run you to the six-oh-six.
**Clive** No, please. On my own. I don't need anyone with me, please.
**Rachel** All right. Can I lend you an alarm clock? Is that allowed?
**Clive** Thank you. You've been marvellous. After my behaviour, I can hardly bear to look you in the face. It's my fault. It's all my fault.
**Rachel** Oh, dear. I'm sorry. This is always happening to me. The more I try and apologize for me, the more other people accuse me of making them feel guilty. This always seems to happen to my relationships.
**Clive** Rachel, you mustn't . . .

**Rachel** (*brusquely*) I must get on. Excuse me. (*She moves away from him to the dining-table with apparently the intention of busying herself there*)

*Clive moves to the hall. Rachel sits at the table sadly*

**Clive** (*pacing the hall*) Oh God, what a mess. What a mess. Why do I do these things? Why, why?

*Belinda comes in along the kitchen passageway carrying a small, very muddy anorak*

**Belinda** The kids are all here. (*She looks into the sitting-room*) Can I bring them through? (*She looks into the dining-room*) Is that all right with everyone? (*With a glance at Clive and Pattie*) Right, I'm bringing them through.

*Belinda goes out*

**Phyllis** What are you going to do, dear?

**Bernard** (*pulling himself to his feet*) Oh, well. The show must go on. The show must go on.

*Bernard starts to straighten his theatre as the Lights fade, and—*

*the* CURTAIN *falls*

SCENE 2

*The same. Very early on the morning of the 27th of December, around 5.15*

*The house is in virtual darkness, lit only apparently by a grey moonlight which is strengthened a little, owing to the fact that outside it is snowing. The areas are all empty except for the dining-room where Harvey in dressing-gown and slippers is asleep in an upright chair, which he has twisted so that, were he awake, he would have a clear view of the hall and front door. On the table beside him is a torch. In his lap, though at present concealed from us by his hands, a loaded revolver. The sitting-room still contains the puppet theatre equipment. This has been stacked as before back in the corner*

*After a moment, a figure is seen creeping down the stairs. It is Bernard, fully dressed, a little bleary. He reaches the hall and listens. It is too dark for him to see Harvey. He goes to the front door, opens it and steps back*

**Bernard** Oh Lord. (*He closes the door*) Fine time to start snowing.

*Bernard goes into the sitting-room. He looks at his theatre rather wistfully. He sits on the arm of the armchair and studies his handiwork thoughtfully*

*In a second, another figure is seen coming from the kitchen carrying a greaseproof package. This time it is Rachel, also fully dressed and wearing a woolly hat and coat. She reaches the hall*

*Bernard hears this and goes to the sitting-room door*

**Bernard** Who's that?

**Rachel** What?

**Bernard** Is that Rachel?

**Rachel** Bernard? What are you doing up so early?

**Bernard** I—er—I couldn't sleep.

**Rachel** Oh.

**Bernard** Well, that's not actually true. I could sleep only Harvey gave us this wretched alarm clock for Christmas, blast him, and it chose to go off at some extraordinary hour.

**Rachel** Oh dear.

**Bernard** Phyllis slept on. So I thought I'd load my stuff. Save time later. But when I saw the snow . . .

**Rachel** (*alarmed*) Snow?

**Bernard** Yes, it's snowing quite hard.

**Rachel** (*going to the door*) Oh damn. Have you seen Clive? Is he up yet?

**Bernard** Clive? No, I don't think so.

**Rachel** I'm running him to the station. We'd better start earlier if it's like this. I lent him my alarm. He should be down by now.

**Bernard** I should have lent him mine. I'm going up again. I won't try and load till this stops. Want me to give him a knock?

**Rachel** Would you? Very quietly. Thanks. I'd better defrost.

**Bernard** Right. (*He moves to the stairs*) You know, it just occurred to me, maybe because it's so early in the morning. I really am a dreadful failure, you know.

**Rachel** Oh no.

**Bernard** Yes. Really and truly.

**Rachel** Is it because of the show yesterday?

**Bernard** Maybe partly that. I mean, let's face it. The poor little blighters were utterly bored to tears, weren't they? I hate to say it but Harvey was right. Absolutely right. He has a thoroughly unpleasant way of putting things but he was right. I really mustn't do any more of them. Enough's enough.

**Rachel** Perhaps you could do something else.

**Bernard** No, no. You get out of touch with children, you see. If you don't have any yourself. Phyllis and I really should have had some but she's so very weak physically, you see. Maybe I should have done something about that but I'm not a very good doctor either. I don't think I've killed anyone mind you. Not to my knowledge. I hope not. But I honestly don't think I've cured many people either. Just left things very much as they were. Oh well. (*He starts up the stairs*)

*At that moment, Clive appears at the top with his case*

**Clive** Hallo.

**Rachel** Clive?

**Clive** Is that Rachel?

**Rachel** Yes.

**Bernard** Good morning.

**Clive** Who's that?

**Bernard** Bernard. I'm just off up.

**Clive** Oh, righto. Goodbye.

**Bernard** (*as they pass on the stairs*) Very nice to have met you. I'll try and read your book when I've a moment.
**Clive** I shouldn't bother.
**Bernard** Really?
**Clive** Really. Bye.

*Bernard goes off upstairs*

*Clive comes down to Rachel*

I said I didn't want you to get up.
**Rachel** Good job I did, it's snowing.
**Clive** Oh no.

*Clive finds his coat on the coat stand and puts it on. Rachel offers him the greaseproof package, still in her hand*

**Rachel** Here.
**Clive** What's that?
**Rachel** Sandwiches.
**Clive** Oh, I don't need . . .
**Rachel** You will on that train. It stops everywhere. You don't get to London till Thursday.
**Clive** Well, thank you. (*He squeezes the packet into his pocket*)
**Rachel** Wait till you see the sandwiches. All my culinary skills to the fore. Took me all last night. Three-inch slices of best white bread. Oh. By the way . . . (*She fumbles in her pocket and produces a balaclava*) It's bound to be freezing too. I brought you this down. Please. Take it.
**Clive** You're sure you don't mind? I mean, it is a woman's balaclava.
**Rachel** It's OK. It's this woman's. (*She smiles*)

*Clive smiles back*

Look, Clive . . .
**Clive** Yes?
**Rachel** There's something I have to say.
**Clive** Ah.
**Rachel** Before you go. What you said yesterday to me about what you felt you thought I felt you needed . . . Well, I think I know why you said it. You said it because of what I'd said to you the night before about what I felt. Didn't you?
**Clive** (*a little uncertainly*) Yes, I think so . . .
**Rachel** About me not being able to give you me because of how I felt.
**Clive** Yes.
**Rachel** Well, the fact is I do.
**Clive** What?
**Rachel** Want to give it. If you want it. You see, I think I only said I didn't want to give it because I felt you didn't want it. I think so. (*A pause*) So . . .
**Clive** I see. Sorry, it's a bit early in the morning to . . .

*A pause*

**Rachel** Well . . . I don't know if that changes anything.
**Clive** (*after a pause, impulsively*) God, I've made such a mess of things.
The story of my life. Look at me. I'm a writer, for God's sake, a writer.
Every time something of value comes along, I . . .

*Rachel sobs loudly*

Now, Rachel, Rachel . . .
**Rachel** (*weeping*) I'm sorry. Getting to be a habit now. I'm beginning to
enjoy it . . .
**Clive** (*feeling in his pockets*) Oh, damn.
**Rachel** What?
**Clive** My new handkerchiefs. I've left them upstairs. I told you. I always
lose handkerchiefs.
**Rachel** Oh, leave them.
**Clive** Not on your life. They're my Christmas present. From you. Hang
on. (*He starts upstairs*)
**Rachel** I'll post them.
**Clive** No.
**Rachel** All right. I'll start the car. I'll be outside.

*Clive goes off upstairs, putting on his balaclava. He leaves his suitcase in
the hall by the Christmas tree. Rachel takes out her gloves, goes to the
front door and out into the snow, jumping in frustration as she leaves,*

*Harvey, in the dining-room, jolts awake*

**Harvey** Huh?

*We see his gun for the first time as he brings it up in a menacing, defensive
gesture. He rises, takes his torch in the other hand and moves to the doorway.
He stops. He flashes his torch briefly on to the suitcase*

My God. (*He hears something on the stairs. He draws back and waits in
the dining-room shadows*)

*Clive comes downstairs cautiously, clutching his box of handkerchiefs*

*As Clive reaches the bottom of the stairs, Harvey steps into the dining-room
doorway, switches on his torch and shines it full on Clive*

All right. Hold it right there. Don't move. I am armed.
**Clive** Oh, dear God. (*He dives for his case*)
**Harvey** I said, stay still.

*Harvey fires a warning shot in the direction of the Christmas tree. There is a
clang as it hits the tub, then the Christmas tree lights come full on and there
is a brisk burst of a children's Christmas song which finishes in a few seconds
with a shrill shriek as the tape snaps evidently damaged by the shot. During
this, Clive grabs his case, holds it up in front of him like a shield and backs
a little way to the door*

**Clive** Don't shoot, you lunatic.

**Harvey** I warned you. (*He fires again*)

*Clive gives one sharp cry. The case flies from his hands, he spins and drops to the floor at the foot of the tree. He lies very still. The Christmas tree lights remain on*

Gotcha.

*A brief silence, then the hall lights flood on*

*Belinda, in night attire, stands at the top of the stairs*

**Belinda** What the hell . . .?
**Harvey** Caught him trying to make off.
**Belinda** Harvey, what have you done?
**Harvey** Picked him off, didn't I?
**Belinda** You fool.

*Neville appears behind her*

You total and utter fool.
**Neville** What's happened?
**Belinda** Look what he's done. Look what this fool's done.
**Neville** Oh, my God. (*He moves down the stairs*)

*Pattie enters at the top*

**Pattie** (*sleepily*) What's happening?
**Neville** Stay there, Pattie. Bel, keep her up there.
**Belinda** You stay here, Pattie.
**Pattie** (*seeing Clive*) What's—oh no. What's . . .? What's . . .?
**Belinda** (*holding on to her*) Come on. Stay here. Stay here. Stay.
**Pattie** I'm—I'm—I'm . . . (*She is getting hysterical*)
**Belinda** (*soothing her*) All right, Pattie, all right. (*To Neville*) How is he?
**Neville** (*who is standing uselessly over the body*) I don't know. I don't know.
   I don't know, do I? (*To Harvey*) You stupid old loony. Where did you
   get that gun?
**Belinda** He's always had it, Nev.
**Neville** I didn't know he had a bloody gun.
**Belinda** You don't know anything, Nev, that's your trouble.
**Neville** How long's he had a bloody gun?
**Belinda** Nev, the man's a walking arsenal. He's got knives and guns and
   God knows what. It's only you who never knew he had a gun. Every-
   body else knew he had a gun.
**Neville** All right, quieten down, Bel. Quieten down.
**Belinda** No good blaming me because he had a gun.

*Eddie enters during the above, also in night attire*

**Eddie** What's happening?
**Neville** There's been an accident, Eddie. Nothing—nothing to worry
   about. Can you take Pattie back to bed, please?
**Eddie** (*seeing Clive*) My God, what's happened down there?
**Neville** (*shouting*) Eddie, will you please take Pattie back to bed, please?

**Eddie** Right. Right.

*Eddie takes Pattie from Belinda and starts to lead her off*

(*To Pattie*) Come on, then, love. Come on, it's all right.

*Pattie and Eddie go off upstairs*

**Neville** Uncle Harvey, would you mind putting that gun down, now? I wish to make a phone call but I'd rather you put that gun down while I'm doing it.

*Harvey, who seems in a sort of daze, does so*

**Belinda** Is he dead?

**Neville** I don't know if he's dead. He's probably dead. That gun's big enough to blow a hole in you the size of a dinner plate.

**Belinda** Oh, dear God.

*Rachel comes in through the front door. She takes in the scene*

**Rachel** (*calmly*) What happened?

**Neville** (*moving over to her*) All right, Rachel. All right. Now, keep calm.

**Rachel** (*looking at Harvey*) Was this him? Did he do this?

**Neville** All right, calmly now. Till we know.

**Rachel** Did you do this?

**Harvey** Look, he was—looting again. He was definitely looting.

**Rachel** He was leaving.

**Harvey** Leaving?

**Rachel** Catching a train.

**Harvey** In a mask? Catching a train in a mask?

**Neville** It's not a mask. It's a balaclava helmet.

**Harvey** Well, they wear those too, some of them. Some of those heavy lads. They wore balaclavas.

**Neville** And some of them probably wore shoes as well. Look, I'm going to phone.

**Rachel** I can't tell if he's breathing. Is he breathing?

**Neville** I don't know, love, I'm not a doctor.

**Belinda** Well, Bernard is. Where's Bernard?

**Rachel** I can't hear him breathing.

*Bernard enters at the top of the stairs with his bag*

**Bernard** It's all right. Eddie told me. It's all right now (*Coming down the stairs*) Let me see him. Rachel, would you just stand away.

**Belinda** Is he alive, Bernard, that's what we want to know. Is he still alive?

**Bernard** Rachel, please would you stand back. Well clear. Thank you. (*He examines Clive*)

**Neville** I'd better phone anyway. (*He picks the phone up*) Oh God, what's the number?

**Belinda** Number of what?

**Neville** The number you're supposed to dial.

**Belinda** What number?

**Neville** My head's gone numb. It's three figures. Come on.

**Belinda** (*puzzled*) Nine-nine . . .

**Rachel** Nine-nine-nine, you mean?

**Neville** Nine-nine-nine. Thank you very much, Rachel. (*Fumbling with the phone*) Look at me. My hands have swollen up. I can't get my bloody fingers in the holes here. (*He puts back the receiver*)

*Bernard stands up gravely*

**Rachel** Well?

**Bernard** (*gravely*) I'm afraid this man is dead. (*A silence*)

**Neville** Oh, dear heaven . . .

**Belinda** (*in a little squeak of anguish*) Oh.

*Rachel walks silently to the front door and looks out*

**Bernard** I'm sorry. (*He moves away*)

*A silence. A moan from Clive*

**Neville** No, he's not, he's still alive.

**Rachel** (*turning swiftly and moving to kneel beside Clive*) He's still alive.

**Belinda** (*hurrying downstairs and also kneeling beside Clive*) Oh, he's still alive.

**Bernard** (*standing alone in agony*) Dear God, what a failure. I can't even get that right. (*He sits on the bench alone and ignored*)

*Clive starts murmuring indecipherably*

**Belinda** He's bleeding a lot.

**Rachel** Yes, but it seems to be his arm or his shoulder. You can't tell. Look, couldn't we run him to the hospital rather than sitting here waiting?

**Belinda** I don't know. Bernard? Bernard?

**Bernard** Yes.

**Rachel** Can we move him?

**Bernard** Don't ask me. I'm the last person to ask.

**Neville** I think we could move him.

**Rachel** We'll risk it.

**Belinda** I'll get some towels.

**Rachel** Yes. Perhaps if we all lifted him, we could—yes, if we use Bernard's station waggon, we could lie him in the back. Bernard?

**Bernard** Yes.

**Rachel** Car key, please. And give us a hand.

**Bernard** (*rising*) All right.

**Neville** Rachel, you take his feet. I'll take this end with Bernard. Bernard . . .

**Bernard** Yes, of course. (*He moves to help Neville. As he does so, he hands Rachel his car keys*) Here. Don't ask me to drive.

**Rachel** No. You'd better come with me, though.

*They begin to prop Clive up between them*

**Neville** All right?

**Bernard** Right.

**Rachel** Right.

**Harvey** (*watching them*) Lot of fuss over a looter, that's all I can say.

*Belinda comes back from the kitchen with a pile of hand towels and tea towels*

**Belinda** Here.

*Clive moans again*

**Bernard** Just a minute . . .

**Belinda** What?

**Bernard** He's saying something. He's trying to say something.

**Belinda** What's he say . . .

**Rachel** Ssh.

**Clive** (*suddenly quite clearly*) I want you. I need you so much. Belinda. Belinda.

*A silence*

**Belinda** He's delirious.

**Rachel** Yes.

**Belinda** He means you. He's got us muddled up. He's saying my name but it's definitely you he wants.

**Rachel** (*flatly*) Yes. Well, it really doesn't matter to me one way or the other.

**Neville** Come on, then. Let's get him in the car.

*Between them Rachel, Bernard and Neville lift Clive and start to take him out through the front door*

Mind his head through the door.

**Belinda** (*following them*) Yes, mind his head.

**Rachel** All right, all right.

*They go out: Rachel, Bernard and Neville carrying Clive, Belinda bringing up the rear with the towels*

*Harvey follows to the front door, leaving his gun behind on the table. He looks out of the door*

**Harvey** Snow as well. That's all we need. All we need is snow.

*Harvey goes upstairs and off*

*Belinda leaps back inside in her bare feet*

**Belinda** Waah! Freezing. (*Looking up the stairs*) That's right, Harvey. You going to lie down then? Good. (*She picks up the suitcase*) Will he want . . . (*She gives up the idea of taking it outside*) Oh. (*She notices that the bullet has in fact drilled a hole right through the suitcase*) Oh.

*Neville jumps back inside also in bare feet*

**Neville** Oooooh!

**Belinda** Look, the bullet went right through his suitcase.

**Neville** Good Lord. Probably saved his life but ruined his laundry. They're taking him down to the Infirmary. I said I'd phone the police.

**Belinda** Do you still have to?

**Neville** Yes. If I don't, the hospital will. You can't go around shooting your guests, you know, whatever you might think of them. He can put that in his book, anyway.

**Belinda** I'm going to make some tea. (*She moves to the kitchen*)

**Neville** Fine. No, you see, the bullet went through the case and . . . (*Something at the base of the Christmas tree catches his attention*) Hallo.

**Belinda** What?

**Neville** (*examining the tub*) It's gone straight through here, see.

**Belinda** Oh yes.

**Neville** Oh, no. He's hit this. (*He pulls out the cassette player hidden in the tub*)

**Belinda** What's that?

**Neville** The kids' Christmas cassette player. The one I rigged for them. (*Opening the lid*) Oh, look at this. (*He puts the machine on the table and pulls away handfuls of loose tape*) What a mess. Looks as if he hit the capstan.

**Belinda** Nev . . .

**Neville** So long as he's missed the motor.

**Belinda** Nev—you going to phone?

**Neville** (*absorbed again*) In a sec. In a sec.

**Belinda** Hey. About Eddie.

**Neville** Yes.

**Belinda** Did you offer him the job with you?

**Neville** Yes, why?

**Belinda** Pattie said you'd offered him manager.

**Neville** Manager?

**Belinda** Of the new branch.

**Neville** You're joking.

**Belinda** You haven't?

**Neville** Not a hope.

**Belinda** She said he swore you had.

**Neville** No. I'd never offer him manager. Not Eddie. He couldn't cope with all that. I told him I was opening a new branch and I'd need staff, that's all.

**Belinda** Oh, that's all right then. I was going to say . . . (*Moving to the kitchen again*) Hope he's all right.

**Neville** Who?

**Belinda** Clive. I hope he's all right.

**Neville** Yes, he'll be all right. He's got Rachel, hasn't he?

**Belinda** Yes. He's got Rachel.

*Belinda goes into the kitchen*

*Neville continues to tinker with the cassette, as the Lights fade and—*

the CURTAIN *falls*

# FURNITURE AND PROPERTY LIST

The following ground plan shows the set in the round as used in the original production. The dining-table and sideboard are chopped in half in a ragged manner as are the floors at the edges of the sitting- and dining-rooms, to give the effect that they continue off-stage. When the puppet theatre is set up in Act II, the armchair is turned round to face it.

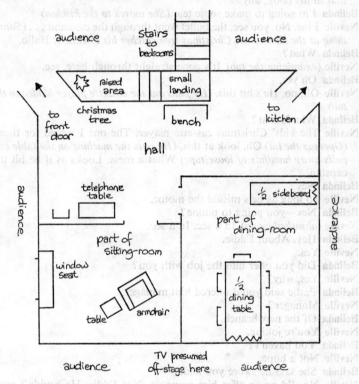

The ground plan below shows the set used in the London production.

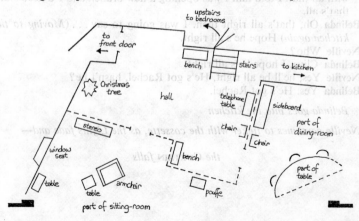

# ACT I

## SCENE 1

*On stage:* HALL:

Small table. *On it:* telephone, table lamp
Upright chair
Wooden bench
Coat and umbrella stand
Radiator
Large Christmas tree in tub. *On it:* partial decorations, light bulbs
with flex, switch and plug. *Around it:* large number of wrapped
and labelled presents including musical drumming bear, wrapped
handkerchiefs in brown paper, pullover, battery-operated vehicle
(half-wrapped). *Concealed in tub:* cassette recorder (hidden
speaker to augment)
DINING-ROOM:
Long table
5 dining chairs
Sideboard. *In it:* bottles of Scotch, ginger ale, empty ginger wine
bottle, assorted glasses, knives and forks (at least 9 of each),
spoons, table napkins, empty ice bucket
Carpet
SITTING-ROOM:
Armchair
Small table
Window-seat
Carpet

*Off stage:* Wrapped presents **(Bernard)**
Boxes of tree decorations **(Belinda)**
Small stepladder **(Belinda)**
9 place mats, flour **(Bernard)**
Small home-made radio remote-control box **(Neville)**
Side plates **(Bernard)**
Bottle of ginger wine, full ice bucket **(Neville)**
Cruet **(Bernard)**
3 open bottles of claret **(Neville)**
Covered serving dish **(Bernard)**
Stack of plates **(Bernard)**
Small suitcase **(Clive)**

## SCENE 2

*Strike:* Ladder
Used bottles, glasses
Everything from long table

*Set:* *On dining-room table:* one or two used breakfast cups, saucers, plates,
clean cups and saucers, dish of cornflakes, spoon, child's monster
annual, paper bag for this, coffee-pot, cream jug, sugar basin
**Bernard's** hat on hall stand
Remnants of sweets over hall floor

*Off stage:* Tray **(Belinda)**
Tray of clean knives and forks **(Neville)**

Puppet theatre, boxes of string puppets (including 3 pigs, dog, wolf, postman), small props, stacks of hand-painted cardboard scenery **(Bernard)**
Damp cloth **(Belinda)**
2 wrapped parcels—chocolates, bottle of Scotch **(Clive)**
Cup of coffee **(Belinda)**
Scarf and boots for **Clive (Belinda)**
Boots for **Clive (Rachel)**
Screwdriver **(Neville)**

*Personal:* **Harvey:** sheath-knife strapped to leg

SCENE 3

**Strike:**  Everything from long table
All empty cups, etc.

*Set:*   *On long table:* snakes-and-ladders board with dice, shaker and counters, used coffee cups and glasses
*On window-seat:* glass of wine (for **Rachel**)

*Off stage:* Tray **(Pattie)**
Pair of very small wellington boots **(Bernard)**
2 hot-water-bottles in ornate covers **(Bernard)**
Glass of water **(Neville)**

*Personal:* **Eddie:** paper hat

# ACT II

## SCENE 1

*Strike:*  Everything from long table
All presents and wrappings from Christmas tree

*Set:*   Any remaining knives and forks in sideboard
*Under Christmas tree:* small red sack with a dozen small gift-wrapped presents
**Bernard's** puppet theatre in working order in corner of sitting-room, pair of scissors nearby
Pig and dog puppets on armchair (for **Pattie**)
*On long table:* cloth, one or two pieces of clean crockery and cutlery, 2 bowls of mousse, bowl of jelly, pieces of clockwork mechanism, box of tools
*Offstage in sitting-room:* copy of *Radio Times*, upright chair

*Off stage:* Cardboard box with paper hats, crackers, squeakers **(Rachel)**
Plate of sandwiches **(Phyllis)**
Plate of sandwiches, covered **(Belinda)**
Plate of chocolate biscuits **(Rachel)**
Pile of paper napkins **(Belinda)**
Cup of coffee **(Rachel)**
Small, muddy anorak **(Belinda)**

*Personal:* **Harvey:** wrist-watch
**Clive:** Father Christmas kit, including beard

## SCENE 2

*Strike:* Everything from long table

*Set:* Puppet theatre equipment stacked in corner of sitting-room
*On long table:* loaded revolver, torch
*In Christmas tree tub:* cassette player with loose tape tangled in it
*On hall stand:* **Clive**'s coat

*Off stage:* Greaseproof paper-wrapped packet of sandwiches **(Rachel)**
Suitcase **(Clive)**
Balaclava **(Rachel)**
**Rachel**'s present of handkerchiefs **(Clive)**
Doctor's bag with instruments **(Bernard)**
Pile of hand towels and tea towels **(Belinda)**

*Personal:* **Bernard:** car keys

# LIGHTING PLOT

Property fittings required: dining-room and sitting-room wall brackets, hall
      pendant, landing light, hall table lamp, Christmas tree bulbs, television
      flicker effect
A hall, sitting-room and dining-room. The same scene throughout

ACT I, SCENE 1  Evening

*To open:* All lights on except Christmas tree and dining-room.
      Television flicker on

| Cue 1 | **Neville** presses control unit button | (Page 12) |
| | *Christmas tree lights on* | |
| Cue 2 | **Belinda** switches off television | (Page 20) |
| | *Fade flicker effect* | |
| Cue 3 | **Belinda** switches off lights | (Page 20) |
| | *Snap off landing and hall lights, retain hall table lamp* | |
| Cue 4 | At end of Scene | (Page 21) |
| | *Fade to Black-out* | |

ACT I, SCENE 2  Morning

*To open:* General effect of bright, cold morning light

| Cue 5 | **Belinda** switches on Christmas tree lights | (Page 22) |
| | *Snap on tree lights* | |
| Cue 6 | **Harvey** switches on television | (Page 31) |
| | *Fade up flicker effect* | |
| Cue 7 | At end of Scene | (Page 37) |
| | *Fade to Black-out* | |

ACT I, SCENE 3  Evening

*To open:* Hall and landing lights on, dining-room lights on, sitting-room in
      darkness, Christmas tree lights on

| Cue 8 | **Belinda** switches off Christmas tree and hall lights | (Page 45) |
| | *Snap off tree and hall lights, retaining table lamp* | |
| Cue 9 | **Clive** switches off dining-room lights | (Page 45) |
| | *Snap off dining-room brackets* | |
| Cue 10 | **Belinda:** "Do you think he's planning to . . ." | (Page 52) |
| | *Christmas tree lights flash on and off* | |
| Cue 11 | **Clive:** "Don't know." | (Page 52) |
| | *Christmas lights on* | |
| Cue 12 | **Clive:** "Yes, look." | (Page 52) |
| | *Christmas tree lights off: repeat on and off as Clive* | |
| | *demonstrates* | |

# EFFECTS PLOT

## ACT I
### SCENE 1

| | | |
|---|---|---|
| *Cue* 1 | **Neville** presses control unit button<br>*Loud Christmas song from concealed cassette player: cut<br>when he presses button again* | (Page 12) |
| *Cue* 2 | **Neville** presses button<br>*Music as above: cut as before* | (Page 13) |
| *Cue* 3 | As **Belinda** moves to dining-room<br>*Front doorbell rings* | (Page 20) |

### SCENE 2

*No cues*

### SCENE 3

| | | |
|---|---|---|
| *Cue* 4 | **Phyllis** switches on battery toy<br>*Augment sound through hidden speaker: snap off when<br>**Clive** stops toy* | (Page 46) |
| *Cue* 5 | **Belinda** throws her arms into Christmas presents<br>*Start up toy effect* | (Page 51) |
| *Cue* 6 | **Belinda:** "Don't touch that one!"<br>*Loud alarm clock rings and Christmas song* | (Page 52) |
| *Cue* 7 | **Clive:** "Who started that bell?"<br>*Cut alarm clock and Christmas song as **Belinda** and **Clive**<br>find control box and clock* | (Page 52) |
| *Cue* 8 | **Clive** stamps on Christmas present<br>*Cut toy effect* | (Page 62) |

## ACT II
### SCENE 1

*No cues*

### SCENE 2

| | | |
|---|---|---|
| *Cue* 9 | **Harvey** fires revolver<br>*Clang, then Christmas song starts up, ending after a few<br>seconds in shrill shriek as tape snaps* | (Page 74) |

MADE AND PRINTED IN GREAT BRITAIN BY
LATIMER TREND & COMPANY LTD PLYMOUTH
MADE IN ENGLAND